0- 1 '70

To/ Mr&Mrs Manthorpe

Thanks for everyth ,

Yvonne&Dennis
xxx

Devonshire Flavour

A Devonshire Treasury
of Recipes and Personal Notes

Collected and edited by
Elizabeth Lothian

David & Charles : Newton Abbot

To Mary Mortimer with gratitude for
her wise and light-hearted encouragement
during the making of this book.

ISBN 0 7153 5396 9

© E. Lothian 1971

First published 1970
Second edition 1971
Second impression 1976
Third impression 1979

Reproduced and Printed in Great Britain by
Redwood Burn Limited, Trowbridge & Esher
for David & Charles (Publishers) Limited
Brunel House Newton Abbot Devon

CONTENTS

iv

COOKING'S
METRICATED DESTINY

When we 'go metric' new recipe books will appear based on the metric units of weight, volume and temperature. In the long interim period we shall continue to use our old and favourite recipes of course; by simple multiplications or with the use of conversion tables we shall bring them up to date; straight conversion may lead to awkward numbers, i.e. 2 oz = 57 grammes, and the nearest convenient quantity will have to be used (60 grammes).

WEIGHT

Pounds and ounces will be replaced by kilogrammes (kg) and grammes (g). 1 kg = 1,000 g = 2·2 lb.

To convert: ounces to grammes multiply by 28·35, grammes to ounces multiply by 0·0352.

Conversion Table

oz	$\frac{1}{4}$	$\frac{1}{2}$	1	2	3	4	6	8	10	12	14
g	7	14	28	57	85	113	170	227	283	340	396

lb	1	2	3	4	6	8	10
g	454	907	1361	1814	2722	3629	4536

VOLUME

Pints and fluid ounces will be replaced by litres (l) and millilitres (ml).

$$1 \text{ pint} = 20 \text{ fluid oz}$$
$$1 \text{ l} = 1,000 \text{ ml} = 1\tfrac{3}{4} \text{ pints}$$

Conversion Table

pint	$\frac{1}{4}$	$\frac{1}{2}$	$\frac{3}{4}$	1	2	3	4
millilitre	142	284	425	567	1134	1701	2268

Note that 1 American pint = four-fifths pint = 16 fluid oz.

1 American cup measure = two-fifths Imperial pint = 8 fluid oz.

1 Scottish gill = $\frac{1}{2}$ pint = 10 fluid oz.

1 English gill = $\frac{1}{4}$ pint = 5 fluid oz.

TEMPERATURE

Degrees Fahrenheit (°F) will be replaced by Degrees Centigrade (°C), (also known as Degrees Celsius). To convert °F to °C, subtract 32, multiply by 5, divide by 9. To convert °C to °F, multiply by 9, divide by 5, add 32, or multiply by 2, subtract $\frac{1}{10}$, add 32.

Conversion Table

The top line gives the gas numbers.

	1/4	1/2	1	2	3	4	5	6	7	8	9
°F	225	250	275	300	325	350	375	400	425	450	475
°C	107	121	136	150	164	178	191	205	219	233	247

Cream—Minimum Milk Fat Content

Clotted cream	55%	Sterilised cream	23%
Double cream	48%	Cream or single cream	18%
Whipping cream	35%	Sterilised half cream	12%
Whipped cream	35%	Half cream	12%

Approximate number of drinks per bottle

Spirits (Gin, Whisky, Rum etc.)	28	glasses
Vermouths, Aperitifs etc.	20	,,
Sherries	14	,,
Ports	14	,,
Table Wines	7	,,
Champagnes, Sparkling Wines	7	,,
Liqueurs	35	,,

Lady Acland

Killerton, Broadclyst, Devonshire.

Sir Richard and Lady Acland live in a flat in Killerton House, once their home, the main part of which is now used as a hostel by students of St. Luke's College of Education, Exeter. Killerton is a National Trust property of about 6,388 acres; it is mainly agricultural and woodland, and the gardens contain an exceptionally fine collection of trees and shrubs. The centre of the 300 acres of park is the Dolbury, an isolated hill with an Iron-age fort. Killerton Clump on the top of the hill has a heronry of twenty to thirty nests.

Lady Acland writes: 'I practise full-time as an architect in Exeter and should not bother to make bread every week if I didn't have an easy recipe. This bread will keep good for a week.'

Easy Brown Bread

3 lb Wholemeal Bread Flour
  (I use Marriage's)
4 teaspoonsful salt
1 oz baker's yeast
Large mixing bowl
Small pudding basin

'Bakewell' paper
2 teaspoonsful sugar
About 2 pints hand-hot water,
  in a jug
3 bread tins
Dripping

Method. Put the flour and salt together in a mixing bowl, and stand this, the bread tins, basin and jug of water in a warm place (I use the plate-warming oven of an Aga cooker for an hour). Everything should be at blood-heat before you start to make the bread. Grease the bread-tins with dripping, and dip them in the flour (or brush with oil, then flour them). In addition I line the bottoms with Bakewell paper.

Cream the yeast and sugar together in the small warm basin and add ½ pint of the water. Put back into the warm place, and watch it until it comes up in a good froth, then pour it all at once into the flour and knead it in, following up with the warm water. Mix it well so that there are no dry patches left: the consistency should be wet and slippery, but not wet enough to pour. The amount of water needed varies with the flour.

Divide up and put into the three tins. Cover with a clean tea-towel, and put back into the warm place. Leave until the dough has risen to within one inch of the top of the tins.

At once put the tins into a hot oven, 475°F, gas 9, reducing after 10 minutes to 425°F, gas 7. Bake for about 1¼ hours.

It is better to over- than under-bake. When done, the sides will ease away from the tin by using a knife and the loaf will slide out.

Cool on a rack.

The Right Hon. Viscount Amory of Tiverton

Pro-Chancellor and Chairman of the Council of the University of Exeter.

'I am capable of boiling an egg and heating a can of soup. I have, however, lately added to my repertoire scrambled eggs or an omelette, whichever it comes out at, and fried sausages.

'My ideal meal I think is eggs or cold ham, home made bread and butter, fresh fruit and coffee or a glass of beer. I doubt whether one can do better wherever one looks.'

> *The country habit has me by the heart,*
> *For he's bewitched forever who has seen,*
> *Not with his eyes but with his vision, Spring*
> *Flow down the woods and stipple leaves with sun,*
> *As each man knows the life that fits him best,*
> *The shape it makes in his soul, the tune, the tone,*
> *And after ranging on a tentative flight*
> *Stoops like the merlin to the constant lure.*
> *The country habit has me by the heart.*
>
> V. Sackville-West, *The Land.*

Lady Amory

Knightshayes Court, Tiverton.

'This is a recipe we are very fond of.'

Chicken Valley of Angel

1 young Chicken	6 oz butter
Half a pint double cream	6 oz Patna rice
Wineglass white wine or cider	1 pint good stock
1 teaspoonful curry powder	1 teaspoonful Worcester sauce

Method. Cut the chicken into eight or ten pieces, depending on the size. Melt 3 oz of the butter in a thick saucepan and after seasoning the chicken fry in the butter until nicely browned on both sides. Put the lid on the saucepan and finish cooking slowly—about 30 to 45 minutes. When ready, remove pieces and keep hot. Drain off a little of the butter in the pan, add the white wine or cider, stir well and boil for a few minutes to reduce. Add cream, Worcester sauce and seasoning. Put chicken back in the sauce and cook for a further five minutes. Serve with curried rice. For that, you melt the remaining 3 oz butter in another saucepan, add the rice and fry until nicely browned, keep stirring, drain off excess fat, add the curry powder and stock, season and cook with lid on until rice has soaked up all the liquid —about 15 minutes. Stir occasionally with a fork. Arrange chicken on serving dish surrounded by the rice which should be dry and each grain separate.

———❖❖❖———

Under the National Gardens Scheme the Gardens at Knightshayes Court are opened to the Public several times during the summer.

Appledore Lifeboat

Miss Moberley, who sent this recipe on behalf of the Appledore life boat crew, is the Honorary Secretary of the Appledore Branch of the Ladies' Lifeboat Guild, was awarded a gold badge in April 1970, for more than 30 years' service to the R.N.L.I. It was presented by Sir Alec Rose, the lone round-the-world yachtsman.

Appledore method of cooking Salmon, to serve cold. This method is used by our fishermen.

Put fish into pan of cold water. Add a couple of spoonsful of oil. Bring to the boil, and boil slowly for 5 minutes. Leave in water to get quite cold.

———❖❖❖———

She writes that in 1825 the Royal North Devon Humane Society started a Lifesaving Boat Station at Appledore, which was not taken over until 1855 by the R.N.L.I. The boat is largely manned by fishermen of Appledore, who net salmon in the estuary.

I am grateful to Captain Lowry of Bideford for information concerning the Lifeboat. In 1962 the late Mr G. B. D. Hawker of Exeter donated the boat in memory of his wife, Louisa Anne. It is a 47 ft Watson type, built by Groves and Gutteridge, I.o.W., number 965, a sister ship of 962, which was lost at Longhope in March 1969 (lifeboats are numbered consecutively). The *Louisa Anne* has a cruising radius of 264 miles, 13 ft beam, $4\frac{1}{2}$ ft draught, displacement $21\frac{1}{2}$ tons; her lifesaving capacity in fine weather is 120, and in bad, 95. She has twin 60 h.p. Gardner diesel engines, with full speed 9 knots, and cruising speed $7\frac{1}{2}$ knots, with normally a crew of seven.

Brian L. Rowsell

Coxswain of Exmouth Lifeboat

Mackerel in Vinegar

Mackerel	Sugar
Butter, oil or fat for frying	Salt and pepper
Large onion	Vinegar

Method. Fillet fish and dry with cloth, then flour and fry until golden brown. Leave to cool.

Place one layer of fillets in bowl and sprinkle liberally with salt and sugar. Place another layer of fish on top and then a layer of sugar and salt. Continue until bowl is full. Take a large onion and cut into thick slices and place over top of last layer. Then pepper all over. Fill bowl with vinegar, cover with lid. Leave for two days then try vinegar. If not to taste, add more sugar. Mackerel prepared in this way will keep for a considerable time.

———❖❖❖———

Exmouth's new Lifeboat the *City of Birmingham* is a Solent Class self righting 48 ft 6 in boat and built of steel. She has two six-cylinder diesel engines, 110 horse power each, giving her a speed of 9 knots. She carries a crew of seven and is fitted with modern wireless and radar. She lies afloat on moorings just off the Harbour entrance. The *City of Birmingham* with a radius of 127 miles, was named in recognition of Birmingham's Lifeboat Appeal, which raised £40,000 after the Longhope disaster.

The Apple-wood Smokers, Totnes

'This is a small firm, running now for six years, and specialising in out-of-the-normal run of smoked foods as well as the usual favourites.'

Smoked Cod Roe

Method.   1. Mix with an equal quantity of butter.

2. To make a milder flavour add an equal quantity of soft breadcrumbs.

3. As an alternative, and for a complete dish, mix with creamed potato, and brown under the grill.

4. Any of the following can be added, with discretion: lemon juice, parsley, thyme, marjoram, garlic, onion, chives, dill, fennel, black pepper, chopped red or green peppers, tomato, cucumber, nasturtium leaves.

Tarama is a smoked roe mixed with lemon juice, olive oil, garlic and black pepper, and smoked again. It may be used as it is, or mixed with cream or cream cheese, or with herbs added, e.g. chives, parsley, lemon balm.

Use for cocktail parties, smorrebrod, sandwiches, canapés, hot or cold patties, hors d'oeuvre, or savouries.

About 1 teaspoonful of powdered mixed herbs, e.g. parsley, thyme, marjoram, bay, will flavour 1 pint of liquid.

Herb Cheese Spread

2 tablespoonsful thick cream
3 tablespoonsful sherry, dry preferably
4 oz grated cheese
Salt and pepper

2 level tablespoonsful mixed fresh herbs, e.g. parsley, sage, thyme, chives, tarragon, etc.

Method.   Mix all together and stir over very gentle heat until the consistency is creamy, and the colour pale green. Put in small hot jars and cover with jam pot covers. Use fairly soon.

'Neatly thatched cornstacks are a rare sight in our countryside today. From a picturesque point of view their passing is sad, for nothing quite replaces them.

'The Devon method of stack thatching is quite different from house thatching. Except for the bottom layer at the eaves, it is put on ear end downwards which is opposite to house thatch. It is fastened with twisted ropes and wooden spears on the outside, whereas the only ties showing on house thatching are at the ridge.

'Nor is rick thatch laid on as thickly, for it is needed to last usually less than a year, and a surprisingly small amount will keep out one winter's rain.

'Making spear sticks is part of the thatcher's craft, an extremely dangerous part, for a very sharp edged tool is needed which is used towards the operator.

'Sticks, usually hazel, ideally about the size of a thick walking stick, are split lengthwise into four, sharpened to a point at each end, then twisted double like hairpins, ready for use.'   H. N. SNOWDON

4

Arlington Court

Arlington Court was given to the National Trust in 1946–47 by Miss Rosalie Chichester, whose family had owned the estate since the fourteenth century. Seven miles north-east of Barnstaple, on east side of the A39, the estate comprises 3,471 acres of hilly country west of Exmoor. There is a two-mile woodland walk by the lake and the river Yeo; buzzards and ravens nest in the woods, and there is a heronry by the lake which is a sanctuary for wild ducks. Shetland ponies and Jacob's sheep graze the steep wooded valleys surrounding the park. The house, designed by Thomas Lee in 1822, is charming, and has much of interest in it; the stables house a large collection of horse-drawn vehicles. We are grateful to the Curator, Mr J. Newman, for allowing access to manuscript recipes used by the family in 1809 and early this century.

Arlington Court Menu

le 10 juin 1910

———

Consommé

———

Sole au gratin

———

Timbales de Volaille

———

Filet de boeuf

———

Meringues

———

Pailles de fromage

Recipes from a 1910 cookery book.

Consomme—clear soup

Marrow bone and chicken bones, previously browned in the oven, covered with water and simmered (1970 note—or in pressure cooker), for two hours, to make 4 pints stock. Allow to get cold.

½ lb shin of beef	½ bay leaf
1 onion	1 carrot
1 stick celery	2 cloves
12 peppercorns	1 sprig thyme
1 sprig marjoram	Sea salt
2 whites of egg	2 egg shells
1 glass sherry	

Method. Remove all fat from the stock. Mince the meat or shred it by scraping downwards with a sharp knife, or cut very small. Prepare the vegetables and cut them into pieces. Whip the whites of the eggs, and crush

5

the shells; put the meat with these, and add to them a tablespoonful of cold water. Put all these ingredients with stock, herbs and spice, into a saucepan. Whisk over a fire until it begins to boil; let it simmer for 10 minutes, then add the wine. Bring it to the boil again, take it off the fire, and let it stand for 5 minutes. Strain through a cloth slowly. Return to the clean saucepan, reheat, season to taste with salt and add a small lump of sugar; it is then ready to serve. Sufficient for six persons.

Sole au Gratin

1 sole	1 shallot
6 mushrooms	1 oz butter
Lemon juice	2 teaspoonsful chopped parsley
Salt and pepper	Brown breadcrumbs
½ gill piquante sauce	

Method. Skin and trim the sole, cut it down to the backbone, and loosen the top fillets without separating them entirely from the bone. Chop shallot and mushrooms, mix them with parsley. Butter a fireproof or gratin dish, sprinkle some of the vegetables and parsley over, place the sole on them, and cover with the rest. Sprinkle with salt and pepper and a squeeze of lemon juice. Cover with brown breadcrumbs, put butter in little bits here and there on the sole. Bake in a moderate oven for about 15 minutes. (Gas 4, 350°F). Remove from oven, pour sauce round and serve.

Piquante—Sharp sauce

4 shallots	3 mushrooms
1 bay-leaf	½ carrot
1 sprig thyme	1 oz butter
½ gill vinegar	½ pint brown stock
¼ teaspoonful anchovy essence	1 tablespoonful Worcester sauce
¾ oz flour	Salt and cayenne

Method. Peel and chop shallots, carrot, mushrooms; melt the butter in a saucepan; fry the vegetables a nice brown; then add vinegar, bay-leaf and thyme. Reduce by simmering to half the quantity of vinegar. Mix flour with a little stock, add rest of stock and contents of pan. Add anchovy essence, Worcester sauce, salt and cayenne. Remove bay leaf and thyme. Return to heat to simmer for ten minutes. Use as required.

Timbales de Volaille—Chicken creams

½ lb quenelle meat	2 oz cooked ham
1 truffle, green vegetables	4 oz cooked chicken
4 mushrooms	1 gill white sauce

1.   Make quenelle meat of chicken or veal. To make chicken quenelle—

¼ lb raw chicken meat	1 oz butter
1 egg	Pepper
½ gill chicken stock	1 oz flour
Salt	Little cream

Method. Cut up the chicken meat, free of skin. Melt butter in a pan, add flour, blend, and add stock, boil until thick, and allow to cool a little. Mix chicken meat and sauce, and pound in a mortar (or liquidiser), add egg and seasoning, mix thoroughly, and sieve if necessary. Add cream.

2. Butter six to eight small moulds, line them carefully with the quenelle meat, leaving enough to cover the tops when filled.

3. Prepare the filling. Cut cooked chicken in small dice. Cook mushrooms in butter, chop truffle, ham and mushrooms, and put with chicken in saucepan. Add white sauce, mix well, and season to taste.

4. Fill centres of moulds with the chicken mixture and cover with the rest of the quenelle meat.

Steam in a steamer, or in a pan of water in the oven, with a greased paper over them for 25 minutes, gas 5, 375°F.

Turn out and dish in a circle, with white sauce over and round, and serve with a green vegetable.

Filet de boeuf

4 lb fillet of beef	Madeira sauce
1 lb mushrooms	Larding bacon
Butter	Vegetables
Salt and pepper	

Method. Trim the fillet by removing the skin and some of the fat; lard it in rows with strips of larding bacon, cut evenly with scissors. Cut some carrots, onions, a small turnip, into pieces and line a deep baking tin with them. Place the fillet on top, season with a little salt and pepper, pour some dripping over, or butter and oil mixed, cover and roast in a moderate oven for one hour, gas 5, 375°F. Baste once or twice during cooking.

Cook the mushrooms in butter, sprinkle with salt and pepper.

Dish the fillet. Warm the sauce, and add some of the gravy from the meat. Pour a little round the meat, garnish with groups of mushrooms. Serve the rest of the sauce separately.

Pailles de Fromage—cheese straws

2 oz flour	1 egg
1½ oz Parmesan cheese (preferably)	½ oz Cheddar cheese
1½ oz butter	Salt and cayenne

Method. Sieve flour into a basin, rub in the butter lightly, grate the Parmesan and Cheddar cheese, mix into flour and butter, add salt and cayenne; mix into a paste with the yolk of the egg and a little water. Turn this paste on to a floured board; roll out into a strip about ⅛ in. thick and 4 inches wide; cut into strips, equal in size. With two cutters, one smaller than the other, stamp out about six rings. Flour a baking sheet, put the straws and rings on it, and bake a golden colour in a hot oven, about 7 minutes, 400°F, gas 6. Serve with straws through the rings.

Marjorie Baker

Colyton.

Mr Baker's Oak Bark Tannery has been in his family for over 100 years, and a Tanyard has stood on this site for 400 years, in Colyton, East Devon. In Britain to-day only about six tanneries exist which still use Oak Bark, preparing the hides by natural means, and by craftsmen, not by machines. The leather produced is more malleable, and is kinder to the wearer and to the craftsmen who prepare the wearing apparel from it. The Ministry of Health insists upon its use, and Mr Baker specialises in sole leather and blocking leather, used for footwear and body belts for orthopaedic work, and he is one of the largest suppliers in the United Kingdom of this special leather to hospitals. He also supplies riding leathers for Great Britain and Eire.

The process takes 9–12 months, and of the hides used, some are Swiss, but most are English.

Supper Dish—bacon, mushroom and egg pie

Method. Line a dish with short crust pastry, then put:—layer of bacon rashers, layer of onion rings (thinly sliced), dot with butter, pour as many seasoned eggs over these, as required, then put:—layer of mushrooms, layer of sliced tomatoes, wrap all in tin foil paper and bake for 45 minutes, 400°F, gas 6.

————— ✦ ✦ ✦ —————

Alternatives

Method. Under the bacon and eggs put a very thin layer of creamy mashed potato—mashed with plenty of butter and milk and well-seasoned. A delicious foundation.

Method. Line dish or plate with pastry, and fill (a) with savoury filling—small tin asparagus, two eggs beaten and poured over the strained asparagus, grated cheese sprinkled over, bake in medium oven 300°F, gas 2, about 20 minutes; or (b) with sweet filling, 1 egg and two tablespoonsful marmalade, beat together, pour on to pastry, and dab with little pieces of butter, bake 300°F, gas 2, about 20 minutes.

Useful for picnics. Non-spilling.

Susan (called Annie) Baker

Exeter,

who has been with the same Devon family for sixty years. She gave these traditional and family recipes, some from her own childhood farmhouse days in East Devon.

Saffron Cake

1½ lb plain flour	3 oz sultanas
3 oz lard	2 oz lemon peel
½ oz yeast	5 grains saffron
½ breakfast cupful caster sugar	½ teaspoonful nutmeg
3 oz currants	Milk—½ pint mixed with water

Method. Put saffron in hot water, stand it where it is warm and let it stay overnight. Rub the lard into the flour, add the sugar, fruit, peel and nutmeg and mix well together. Put the yeast into a basin, sprinkle small teaspoonful of caster sugar over.

Take half a teacupful of milk and water, add the yeast, stir this up and sprinkle a little flour on the top. Put this in a warm place and allow it to rise. When sufficiently risen take ½ pint milk and ½ pint warm water including the water strained from the saffron. Add the yeast mixture and the saffron to the flour, fruit, etc. and mix all together. Cover with a cloth and put in a warm place to rise. (This may take 1½ hours).

Take the risen mixture from the basin and put into baking tins and put in warm place to rise nearly to top of tins.

Bake in fairly hot oven 425°F, gas 7 until brown, then cool off. (In 1970, 10 grains saffron cost 3s. in an Exeter Chemist's).

Leek Pie (*to go with cold meat*)

For two—Short pastry, two good sized leeks.
Method. Wash leeks and cut into one inch pieces. Boil in milk and add pepper and salt. Put in pie dish, add a little cream, cover with pastry and bake in oven until pastry is done.

White Turnip Pie (*to go with cold meat, after golf, especially in winter*)

Method. Cook turnips in milk, mash well, add cream, salt and pepper, place in pie dish, cover with pastry and cook.

Ginger Wine

To every gallon of water add:

1½ Seville oranges	1½ lemons
1½ lb good raw sugar	1½ lb lump sugar
2 oz root ginger (bruised)	8 oz raisins

Method. Boil sugar, ginger and half the fruit peel for three-quarters of an hour, keeping it well skimmed. When cold, add the juice of lemons and oranges and the remainder of the peel.

Put some fresh yeast on toasted bread to float on the top of the tub or pan and ferment 24 hours. Chop the raisins and put in the pan or tub. Stir it every day till it stops fermenting. Put in what brandy you think proper.

Rachel and Jim Beesley

Castle Inn, Lydford.

Rachel was Domestic Science teacher at the Girls' Grammar School, Torquay and Jim was Further Education Officer for Devon from 1947 to 1964 when he retired and bought the Castle Inn. (It hasn't been retirement, but it has been 'Further Education'!).

The Castle Inn is next to Lydford Castle, a stannary prison dating from 1195; it is near the famous Lydford Gorge, and close to one of the loveliest parts of Dartmoor. It has a great Norman fireplace. The village was once a Saxon borough with its own mint, and long before that, was important when Mediterranean civilisations were seeking tin for their bronzes.

Devon Roast

This is a way of cooking the 'Sunday Joint' or small pieces of meat, chops, etc. This method calls for the minimum amount of attention during cooking.

Joint of pork, lamb or beef, or lamb or pork chops, braising steak, liver and bacon. Root vegetables, potatoes, onions, carrots, parsnips.

Method. Weigh meat and assess time as for roasting.

Put into a roasting pan, sprinkle with salt, pepper and flour.

Cover bottom of pan with water to a depth of 1–2 inches. Place in oven 400°F or gas 6.

Prepare vegetables and parboil for 5 minutes. Add to meat in pan, allowing 1½ hours for cooking vegetables. Sprinkle vegetables with flour.

N.B. Vegetables and small pieces of meat are put in pan at the same time.

At the end of the cooking period vegetables will be brown and the meat cooked. Remove from dish. Thicken the remaining gravy and add browning if necessary.

Raw Fry

This is a delicious vegetable accompaniment to bacon or gammon rashers and sausages.

Method. Cook bacon or sausages in a frying pan. Remove from pan and keep warm.

Prepare and slice thinly potatoes and onions, two-thirds potatoes to one-third onions.

Add potatoes and onions to the pan, add salt and pepper and if liked, flour and browning to thicken.

Cover with lid, and cook over a low heat for 20–30 minutes, until softened.

Serve on dish surrounded by bacon or sausages—keep hot. Fry eggs and serve on top of vegetables.

Joy Bennett

Mrs Bennett is the wife of the Town Clerk of Exeter. She finds that her 'family enjoys this cake, particularly at Christmastime. Its light texture and "tangy" flavour are a welcome change from rich Christmas fare.'

Cranberry Cake

7 oz sugar	8 oz plain flour
3½ oz margarine	2 teaspoonsful baking powder
1 egg	¼ teaspoonful salt
½ teaspoonful vanilla essence	6 tablespoonsful milk
4 oz fresh cranberries (halved)	1–2 tablespoonsful caster sugar

Method. Cream margarine and sugar together. Add egg and blend, beating well. Fold in dry ingredients together with milk and vanilla essence (added to milk). Fold in cranberries and turn into an 8 in. greased square tin. Sprinkle top with caster sugar, and bake in moderate oven, 350°F, gas 4, for about 50 minutes.

———— ❖ ❖ ❖ ————

The Reverend William Keble Martin lived at Woodbury, near Exeter. In his famous and beautiful Concise British Flora in Colour, he illustrates the cranberry, which lives on wet boggy heaths, and could be encouraged to grow on Dartmoor. Devon's wild berry, the whortleberry, grows on Dartmoor, and many people go gathering the 'worts' in August, to make fruit pies.

Joan S. Blacksell

wife of the Headmaster of Barnstaple Secondary Modern School.

Ham and Apple

Apples! The best of English dishes incorporate apple in some form, especially in the West Country. Apple pie is best of all, but most people have a favourite way of doing that. This savoury dish is worth a trial.

Slices of ham (about ¼ in. thick)	Large cooking apples
Demerara sugar	Lemon juice

Method. Peel and core some large apples and cut into rings. Take a dish of suitable size and make layers—a slice of ham, apple rings overlapping to cover it, a sprinkle of sugar. Continue until a sufficient quantity is used (this dish is equally good for a small or large party) finishing with a slice of ham. Squeeze the juice of a lemon over all and give a final sprinkle of sugar. Cover and cook in a moderate oven for ½ an hour, uncover and cook in a fairly hot oven for another ½ hour or until the juices thicken. Serve with roast potatoes or any vegetables.

Mrs Arthur Boxall

Teignmouth Chicken Casserole

1. Cut a 3½ lb roasting chicken into 4 or 5 pieces. Roll each piece in seasoned flour, and sear in oil and butter until golden.
2. Remove from the pan, and in the same fat fry quickly, 2 oz chopped mushrooms, 2 oz shallots and 2 oz diced bacon.
3. Place the chicken on top of these three, and pour over, 1 pint dry cider. Add a pinch of cinnamon, 1 bay leaf, a sprig of thyme and 1 clove of garlic.
4. Allow the cider to boil and place in an ovenware casserole.
5. Braise the chicken, covered, gas 6, 400°F, for about 40 minutes. Remove from oven, lift out chicken pieces, and keep hot on a dish.
6. Thicken the sauce with a compound paste of 2 oz flour blended with 2 oz margarine, and add in small pieces to the stock in the casserole.
7. Bring to the boil and simmer for 5 minutes. Pour over the chicken and serve at once. Garnish with fingers of fried bread.

———— ✦ ✦ ✦ ————

A Devon Maid

'I was born in Teignmouth, educated at Maynard School, Exeter, and my sister, brother and I had a happy Christian childhood. We spent long days sailing, and walking on Dartmoor, just as my father, Ernest Radford had spent his boyhood. Later, without moving away very far, I married a bank clerk, and except for the anxious war years, history repeated itself. Our four children spent their childhood sailing, and walking on the moor. After they grew up and left home, I achieved a lifelong ambition, and qualified as a nurse, spending several years nursing in a Geriatric Hospital in Exeter. Now I seem to have a full-time occupation as a grandmother, which involves among other activities, going out to the Cayman Islands to housekeep for one of my daughters-in-law, when another grandchild arrives at midsummer.

'Soon my husband will retire from the bank, and we are moving to a village deep in the countryside, the very heart of Devonshire, with woods nearby, for the dogs and us to walk in, and it will be a very satisfying life.

'Our forebears sailed in the Clippers, and my father's ancestors have all been Devon men.'

Miss Doris M. Bradbeer

Topsham, Devon.

Governor of Maynard School, Exeter; Member of Exeter Y.W.C.A. Development Committee; Trustee, Woodhayes Eventide Home, Exeter.

Apricot Cake

8 oz self-raising flour	4 oz butter
4 oz caster sugar	2 standard eggs
4 tablespoonsful apricot jam	1 oz split almonds
1 dessertspoonful caster sugar	A few drops almond essence
	Pinch of salt

Method. Put flour and salt in a bowl. Rub in butter. Stir in sugar. Beat egg with almond essence. Stir in egg and jam together. Put in a greased tin and smooth over top. Cover with almonds and sprinkle the dessertspoonful of sugar over. Bake below centre of oven, gas 3, 325°F for 1 hour and 10 minutes. Cool in tin 15 minutes.

———— ❖ ❖ ❖ ————

'The Romans came to Topsham as early as A.D. 50, and here, on the banks of the river Exe, near where Retreat House now stands, they probably found one of the rural communities which were a feature of English life at that time, with centres in London, York, Chester, Gloucester and Exeter, each community run by local tribunals for the dispensing of laws and justice.

'This method of government was quite highly developed, and therefore acceptable to the Romans, who were content to supervise, and keep a watching brief.

'Topsham became the port for Isca Dumnoniorum (Exeter), and a naval base, supplemented by a straight road running parallel to the river from Topsham to South Street, Exeter.

'Topsham has held a Fair for the three days of the Festival of St Margaret in July since 1257, when Henry III declared it a town, not a village . . . it carried on a larger business than any other port outside London. Sea-borne trade was greatly increased when, in consequence of a dispute between Isabella, Countess of Devon, and the City Fathers in 1284, over the sale of fish, the Courtenays dammed the river Exe at Countess Weir, thus obstructing the passage of all ships up the river. Vessels bound for Exeter were forced to unload their cargoes at Topsham Quay, whence the merchandise was carried to Exeter by road. In 1280, while Exeter Cathedral was in course of construction, some of the stone brought from Purbeck was unloaded at Topsham and conveyed to Exeter by bullock cart.'

From *The Story of the Manor and Port of Topsham*, by D. M. Bradbeer.

Peggie de Brett

Honiton.

President, Exeter Art Society.

'Being a keen amateur painter, gardener, etc. etc., I always choose recipes that need as little preparation and attention as possible.'

Sweet and Sour Casserole

This cooks itself in a slow oven, for an almost indefinite time, whilst you paint, dig or play Schubert's Sonatas. Pork or Lamb chops in a Pyrex dish, covered with sliced tomatoes, a little tomato sauce, brown sugar, lemon juice and a few slices of lemon, salt and paprika.

Blackberry Muesli—for 4 people

This came originally from Switzerland, I believe, but I picked it up in Alderney. It can be made with any fruit.

3 oz quick-cooking oats (approx.)
1 lemon (juice and grated rind)
2 cupsful stewed blackberries
1 chopped banana

1 grated apple
Some chopped walnuts
¼ pint raw cream or condensed milk

Method. Mix thoroughly, and if it seems too stiff, add more fruit juice. Best left in frig. for a few hours. *'This is quite delicious and fattening.'*

Cheese Sauce

1 oz butter or margarine
½ pint cold milk
Seasoning

1 oz plain flour or corn flour
Pinch cayenne
2 or 3 oz cheese

Method. Melt fat over low heat, add flour, cook 2 minutes without browning. Gradually add milk, stirring until smooth. Stir carefully until boiling. Add cheese, grated or thinly sliced with a potato peeler, stir until it has blended. Add pinch cayenne pepper if liked.

'She's a true Devonian; if there's anything she hates, it is to be committed to a definite statement.'—John Galsworthy, 'A Man of Devon'.

Ursula W. Brighouse

Woodbury.

'I first met this recipe in Woodbury, and have not come across it anywhere else. It is quick and easy to make, cheap as party sweets go, can be made the day before, and uses the yolks as well as the whites. Besides my hobbies of cookery and music, I am greatly interested in natural history and local history. Woodbury is an excellent place to pursue these hobbies; the Common and well-treed farmlands are rich in bird and flower life. There is history in every corner of the parish, to Saxon and even earlier times. I can't think of a pleasanter place to live than Woodbury.'

Cloud Pie

Four to six portions.

For the case:

3 egg whites	6 oz caster sugar
¼ teaspoonful cream of tartar	

For the filling:

3 egg yolks	6 oz caster sugar
2 large lemons	¼ pint double cream

Method. Grease a large baking tray with good oil or pure lard. Cover with a sheet of well-greased paper and dust lightly with cornflour. Whisk egg whites till dry-stiff, add cream of tartar and whisk again, then add sugar in three lots, whisking well in between. Mixture should now be very stiff indeed with no signs of wetness in handling.

With a spatula, shape the meringue into a flan case on the baking tray, pulling the mixture from the centre and shaping a smooth even wall 1½ inches high. Dredge lightly with caster sugar to prevent spreading, and place in moderately hot oven, 350°F, gas 4. for 2 or 3 minutes. Transfer to very cool oven, 130°F, very low gas, and bake for 2 hours. Peel paper off carefully, and cool on flat surface.

Place egg yolks, sugar, lemon juice and grated rind in double pan, whisk lightly and cook gently till consistency of lemon-curd. Cool, whip cream and beat in to lemon mixture. Fill case, and refrigerate 12 hours.

Meringues

3 whites of eggs	6 oz caster sugar

Method. Whisk egg whites until the bowl can be held upside down without them slipping. Fold in sugar carefully. Lightly oil grease proof paper. Put the mixture out, a dessertspoonful at the time. Dust lightly with caster sugar and place in a very cool oven until dry. If necessary, turn them over and return to the oven until dry right through. Makes 16–18 shells. Fill when needed with whipped cream, putting two shells together.

Paddy Brimacombe

Topsham, Devon.

Member of Y.W.C.A. Development Committee.

Paddy Brimacombe works hard and very happily for several good causes. She has lived in Devon for over 35 years and wouldn't live anywhere else. The Christmas Puddings and Marmalade are 'best sellers' at Coffee Mornings, and even on the 'Eats' stall at Jumble Sales.

Christmas Puddings—a very old family recipe

½ lb beef suet
½ lb raisins
½ a grated nutmeg
1 wineglassful brandy (a big one)
½ lb sultanas
1 lemon and 1 orange (juice and grated rind)
Pinch of salt
Large grated carrot

2 oz flour
¼ lb mixed peel
1 teaspoonful mixed spice
½ lb breadcrumbs
¼ lb currants
3 eggs
2 oz chopped almonds
6 oz Demerara sugar
Few chopped dates

Method. Skin the suet and chop it finely. Clean fruit, stone the raisins. Finely shred the mixed peel. Squeeze the lemon and orange and grate the rinds.

Put all the dry ingredients in a basin and mix well.

Add lemon and orange juice. Stir in eggs one at a time and add the brandy.

Work the whole thoroughly for some minutes till well blended and leave overnight.

Tie down in well greased basins and boil—big puddings for about 8 hours and small ones for about 5 hours. Reheat for 2 hours.

All-the-year-round Marmalade

2 grapefruits
2 large oranges
6 lb sugar

2 lemons
6 pints water

Method. Finely shred fruit rinds and place with the juice and water in preserving pan and simmer till tender. Add sugar and boil till it jells, i.e. about 1 hour. A good 'walnut' of butter in the pan will prevent burning.

This recipe will give you about 12 lb delicious marmalade.

A Supper Dish—*that can be prepared in the morning and forgotten till half an hour before it is to be eaten.*

1 large tin celery hearts
1 pint really good cheese sauce

6 hard boiled eggs—halved
A little grated cheese to sprinkle on top

Put celery hearts and eggs in an ovenproof dish and cover with the cheese sauce. Sprinkle with the grated cheese. Bake at moderate temperature for about 30 minutes.

British Red Cross Society

Mrs A. T. Soper, Divisional President, Exeter.

The British Red Cross Society celebrated its centenary in 1970. There are now 113 recognized Societies, with a membership of two hundred and twenty million.

Group members give service, and Associates contribute financially. Help is welcomed in all sections.

Creamed Salad Ring

1 tablespoonful gelatine	1 pint tomato juice (or one large
¼ pint milk or evaporated milk, or	can of cream of tomato soup)
double cream	Salad, shrimps, mayonnaise

Method. Dissolve powdered gelatine in some very hot tomato juice or soup. Add to rest, and when cool but not set, whisk in the milk or cream. Season well. Pour into ring mould, and when set turn out. Fill centre with green salad, shrimps and mayonnaise.

Miss Theo Brown

Honorary Research Fellow in British Folklore, University of Exeter; Recorder for Folklore, Devonshire Association; Member of Committee, The Folklore Society (London).

The following is the recipe used by my father, H. Langford Brown, of Barton Hall, Kingskerswell, Devon.

My father constructed a special brick kiln in an outbuilding, and I can remember how good the results were, so I hope the recipe given is as accurate as it is extravagant for these days !

To Cure Four Hams

Method. Boil together for 20 minutes in four gallons of water, 6 lb of bay salt, 4 lb coarse brown sugar, 4 oz of saltpetre, 6 oz black pepper, bruised and tied in muslin. 2 lb common salt and 3 lb brown treacle; add when cold, 4 pints strong beer.

Soak hams in this for a fortnight, and then smoke in a chimney for 3 weeks, but if in a kiln, for 8 days. Only wood must be burnt in the fire, and if you smoke in a kiln, sawdust is best. My father does not specify the wood, but I am sure he used oak-sawdust.

Ian Browning

Exeter.

Mr Browning's family of fish merchants have been merchants in Exeter for over 200 years.

Dressed Crab and Salad

2 hard-boiled eggs, parsley

Method. Wash crab shell and polish with a little oil. Hit shell sharply at natural line to remove. Break centre in half, remove meat from crevices, being careful not to get small pieces of shell as well. Smash claws, and keep white flesh separately in a small basin. Mix soft breadcrumbs with dark meat, add mayonnaise, or cider vinegar or lemon juice, to taste.

Fill each end of the crab shell with white meat, and put dark meat in middle. Sieve hard-boiled egg yolks, and chop whites separately. Hold knife-blade edge along the join of white and dark meat, and make a band of egg yolk neatly against it, on either side; inside each band, on the dark meat, make a line of chopped egg whites. Sprinkle a line of chopped parsley outside each yellow band.

Place crab on lettuce leaves, garnish with halved tomatoes. If coral is available, blend with butter and pipe small rosettes on the crabmeat, round edge of shell. Serve with thin slices of brown bread and butter.

Crab and Salad

Method. With a fork mix the body and claw meat gently in a basin, and blend in about 2 oz double cream, a little mustard freshly mixed with milk, salt and pepper, the juice of half a lemon, and about a teaspoonful cider vinegar. Put the mixture aside for half an hour to blend flavours. After a final stir, using two teaspoons, put small helpings inside the curved inner leaves of a well-hearted lettuce. Eat preferably with brown-bread rolls, farm butter, lettuce, tomatoes and spring onions (if in Devonshire, 'chibbles' or 'chipples').

Choose fresh crabs, feeling heavy in the hand. If they rattle when shaken they contain water, so choose others. The claws should be springy, not droopy. Discard the inedible stomach, intestines, and the gills, which are the sixteen 'dead men's fingers', and are grey in colour.

Crabs are available in South Devon from March to December. In spring the cock is a better buy: later, about August to September, the hen is better, as that is spawning time, and the coral is present. The cock crab has a narrower 'flap' of shell than the hen.

Mrs K. R. Bryant

President of Torquay Y.W.C.A., and also President Torbay Division of the British Red Cross Society and Chairman since 1959 of Hospital Management Committee of fifteen Hospitals, among other appointments.

Westcountry Pasty

Pastry:

1 lb plain flour	4 oz lard
4 oz margarine	Salt, pepper, water to mix

Filling:

1 lb beef skirt	3 onions
4 large potatoes	

Method. Roll pastry to tea-plate size, about 6 in. Cut onions, meat and potatoes. Put a layer of potatoes, onions and meat on pastry. Pinch up edges to shape and close top of pasty. This makes about 10 pasties.

Oven No. 5, 375°F, after 20 minutes wash over with milk, then continue cooking for an hour, 20 minutes on top shelf, 20 minutes on middle, and 20 minutes on lowest shelf. Put a lump of butter on each.

———— ✧ ✧ ✧ ————

Torbay Royal Regatta 1934

'Since Sandpiper naturally had none of her species with which to compete I sailed with Maxey in his new Bermuda-rigged boat, which was a marvel in light winds, her mast being twice as long as the boat. The place which her name should have occupied in the programme was filled by a dash, for partly on account of her habits and partly because of her scarlet sail, she was known locally as "Bloody Mary", a title which the Committee refused to print. She got even more lurid titles than that, by the outer mark buoy. We were ahead of the whole field when the wind strengthened bringing the two nearer boats, which were heavier, to overhaul us. It is an immutable law of the sea that boats overtaking keep clear of the overtaken, so we held on to cut the buoy by half a yard. Capt. — overhauled on the inside, wishing to cut closer to the buoy than ourselves, but our course forced him either to give way or to pass on the wrong side of the buoy. His boom swung across us and the boats crashed, nearly knocking me from the helm. The wind and the seas were boisterous but the language was even more so. A loyal crew they were and their language shook the Captain's nerve, for he went off the wind afterwards and we sailed to victory in spite of being fouled....

'The afternoons are occupied by athletic events ... but we in company with other boats, spent the afternoon in Paignton Harbour arguing disgracefully over the division of prize money ... a traditional procedure.... Did not Frobisher say of Drake when he got to harbour after the defeat of the Armada, "He thinketh to cozen us of our share of the ducats, but we will have our share or I will make him spend the best blood in his belly"....

'By evening we had re-cemented our friendship by drinking ... the outstanding sum in question, in the New Pier Inn.'

Under sail through red Devon, Raymond B. Cattell.

Professor John Caldwell

Head of the Department of Botany in the University of the South West, later the University of Exeter, 1935–1969, and now he and his wife are joint Wardens of Hope Hall, a mixed hall of residence in the University.

Roast Pigs Trotters

2 pigs feet and one pigs knuckle (unsalted), for two persons
Stock, parsley, salt and pepper   ½ oz plain flour
Get the butcher to chop the knuckle in two.

Method. Prepare the trotters by scraping and singeing any bristles and cleaning under the cold tap. Place in heavy metal pan, cover with cold water or stock and salt to taste. Bring to boil and either simmer on stove or place in low oven for 2½ hours approx. When the meat is coming away from bones, make a smooth paste with plain flour in another saucepan. Pour hot pork stock gradually into paste, stirring briskly, using about ½ pint liquid.

Arrange the drained trotters and knuckle in pan and roast in top of very hot oven for about 45 minutes.

Flavour thickened pork stock with parsley, salt and pepper and serve as accompanying sauce. Serve potatoes and swede turnips mashed together with butter and pepper. If you wish to have greens, curly kale is a perfect complement to this rich dish. We also have a bowl in the middle of the table to place the masses of bones in as we are eating.

Until 1947 Professor Caldwell was in charge of the College Estate and during the war was responsible for the food production carried out in the fields and gardens. Poultry, rabbits, goats and pigs were reared to help with the feeding of the college residents and while pork was rationed strictly, the offal was not! The above recipe, a nourishing and appetising one, was used.

'Village thatchers of the past usually boasted a second skill, perhaps wisely as if it were a second string to their bow. Often sheepshearing was the other craft, probably because around hot midsummer is a slack time for thatching but ideal for shearing. Maintaining shears in good order is no mean skill, for cutting fine sheepswool requires perfect shear edges.

'I well remember the old thatcher who sharpened mine when, as a youth, I was learning to shear. Several years I watched his huge horny and gnarled hands holding the edges to the grindstone while I turned the handle for him.

'Eventually at a great age when his fingers were becoming fumbly he said, with soft spoken, kindly voice, "Now you've seen me do it enough times, you can do it as well as I can".

'The door he opened for me was closing for him.'

H. N. SNOWDON.

The Lady Caradon

Trematon Castle, Saltash, Cornwall.

The Lady Caradon, Trematon Castle, Saltash, is a close neighbour, and a good friend to Devon.

'*Born in Italy of a Scottish father and an Italian mother; educated in Florence at the Poggio Imperiale. Childhood spent in Baghdad, Edinburgh, Florence, Bologna. As a young woman accompanied her parents to Palestine, where her father was adviser to the Oil Companies. There she met Hugh Foot (now Lord Caradon), son of Isaac Foot of Callington, Cornwall. They were married in Haifa —their first son was born there, their daughter in England, a third son in Jamaica, and their last son in Lagos, Nigeria. A lifetime spent in many parts of the world, and a particular interest in the national dishes of all these countries, have made her appreciate not only what is delicious, but what is also easy to serve. Here is a mouth-watering dish for a cold supper, fit for gourmets, but requiring only the use of one plate and one fork for each person. Once the dish is set on the table there is no need for any one to move from the table at any time! The thing to do is to dig deep into it and have at least two helpings!*'

Chicken and Ham Salad

1 cold boiled chicken
1 packet frozen French beans
1 packet frozen peas
2 or 3 large potatoes
2 cupsful of pure olive oil in a small jug
The juice of 1 lemon
2 very thick slices of ham, weighing 4 oz each
2 or 3 large carrots
The separated yolks of 2 very fresh eggs

Method. Boil the beans, peas, carrots and potatoes, *separately.* When they are cooked and rather firm, put them, each in a separate saucer or plate, and leave them in a cool place to chill.

Cut all meat off the boiled chicken and slice it into small cubes of about 1 in.

Cut the slices of ham into cubes and mix the cubes of ham and chicken together. Put on one side to chill thoroughly.

Now you are ready to make your mayonnaise thus: Stir the 2 yolks of egg in a pudding basin, with a wooden spoon till creamy. The eggs must not have even a vestige of white in them.

Now drop five drops, not more, of olive oil from your little jug into the yolks, and continue to stir till the oil is completely incorporated in the egg. Continue to do this, with two or three additional drops each time, never ceasing to stir. When the mixture becomes firmer, one may be bolder in adding the oil. One cup of oil per yolk will be necessary, sadly expensive, but delicious! The mayonnaise will become stiffer and stiffer until it becomes like a solid ball. Now add the juice of one lemon, a very little at a time, stirring continually. The mayonnaise will become slightly paler and more liquid. Add two pinches of salt and taste. The mayonnaise is ready and all trace of taste of olive oil has vanished. (If you have a blender, it will save your wrist! Make *it* stir the mayonnaise, but you still have to drop in the oil. Careful!)

Take a deep crystal or Pyrex bowl and toss a layer of the chicken and ham cubes (half of what you have) in the bottom of the bowl. With your wooden spoon smear a layer of mayonnaise on this. Then a layer of mixed sliced carrots and peas, and another thin trace of mayonnaise. Then a layer of cold sliced potato, topped by a layer of cold French beans and a final dressing of mayonnaise, using up all the mayonnaise. Your dish is ready. Stick a pair of wooden salad servers in the midst of the dish and put it firmly down on the table. It is a rich dish, with plenty of meat, lots of vegetables, and the tangy taste of good home-made mayonnaise.

This is a complete meal—no other courses can possibly be required. A glass of chilled white wine goes down very well with this.

<hr>

Ratatouille—vegetables.   For 6–8 people.
This can be prepared the day before: it can be eaten hot or cold, and can be re-heated.

2 aubergines peeled or unpeeled, cut into strips	2 onions chopped
	2 sliced green or red peppers
1 lb firm ripe tomatoes, peeled	2 small courgettes, or a piece of
Salt and pepper	marrow, cut up
2 cloves crushed garlic	Oil for frying

Method.   Cover the bottom of a pan with oil, add chopped onion and, when beginning to soften, add other vegetables and seasoning. Cover and simmer for about 30 minutes. Remove lid and continue cooking until the vegetables have absorbed the oil.

Almond Petit Fours
These quantities make about 60:

4 oz ground almonds	1 oz butter
6 oz caster sugar	Egg white (use half)
Few drops Noyau (if liked)	

Method.   Beat butter, sugar and ground almonds together, add Noyau if used, and pound all together with egg white. Take pieces the size of a large garden pea, and roll into small balls. Place an inch or two apart, on lightly oiled greaseproof paper on baking sheet. Bake 7–10 minutes until pale brown, 350°F, gas No. 4. Leave a moment or two before removing to a wire tray.

Stella Chesterfield
Exeter.

Apple Chutney

1 quart vinegar (cyder vinegar preferably)	2 lb apples
	1 lb raisins
1 lb brown sugar	1 oz mustard seed
1 lb onions	2 teaspoonsful salt
1 teaspoonful cayenne pepper	

Method. Chop all ingredients, boil for one hour, or until tender, put into hot jars, and seal.

————◆◆◆————

Apples are native to Britain, and were an important fruit crop in prehistoric times. They were cored, cut into rings, dried and stored. The sugar in the dried fruit would have made them palatable. Edwards Hyams in *The Speaking Garden* considers it possible that orchards were planted in Neolithic times, and that apples were cultivated first, for cider-making. He also thinks it probable that the apple is the only fruit to have spread from west to east. Later it went from France and Britain to the Americas, and from Britain to Australia and New Zealand.

Cider-making has continued in Devonshire for centuries. Professor Hoskins writes in his book *Devon*, 'On the Earl of Devon's manor of Exminster, the bailiff's account for the year 1285–86 shows cider-making on a considerable scale', and 'In Elizabethan days cider—especially from the coastal parishes—was sold in large quantities for the provisioning of ships.'

About 1724, Defoe wrote that between Topsham and Axminster so much fruit grew, and so much cider made that 'sometimes they have sent ten and twenty thousand hogsheads a year to London'. (One hogshead = 52½ imperial gallons.)

The old methods survive on farms, of using hand or horse presses. Mrs Brighouse of Woodbury edits a village monthly magazine covering all aspects of village life and activities, and while researching into the history of cider-making there, found that 'five private cider presses still operate in the village, mostly on farms that still have their old cider apple orchards'.

————◆◆◆————

'Devonshire cream is also of great antiquity. We learn this incidentally from the fact that the dairies on the Tavistock Abbey estates in the early fourteenth century had no churns for butter-making, but raised the famous clotted cream by scalding the milk. The cream, when cold, was then stirred and butter produced in that way. The monks of Tavistock and their tenants were certainly familiar with clotted cream as a result of this process. Indeed, the process is so simple as to suggest that it was known in prehistoric times.' PROFESSOR HOSKINS, *Devon.*

The Ministry of Agriculture, Fisheries and Food Advisory Leaflet No. 438 on Clotted Cream says that 'The butterfat is firm and of very good colour when the cows are fed on good grass. Nowadays a considerable amount of clotted cream is made in West Country creameries, and the quality is uniform and good, although some of it may lack the finer points of the best farm-house product.'

Agatha Christie

Churston Ferrers, Brixham, South Devon.

I enclose the only ones I can think of at the moment. They are at any rate true Devonian recipes of my childhood. I was born in Devon and am still more at home there than anywhere else in the world.

Devon Squab Pie

6 mutton cutlets, best end of neck	Onions
Apples	Hard-boiled eggs

Method. Lay cutlets on bottom of pie-dish. Sprinkle over with finely chopped onion (or thinly sliced if preferred).

Lay on a layer of thinly sliced apples. Cover with stock and seasoning.

Cook in slow oven until apple-and-onion is cooked, and meat. Add six halved hard-boiled eggs, and cover with pastry brushed with milk. Return to oven until pastry is cooked.

Note: It used to be said that if the wife ruled the household a sprig of rosemary should be added. If the master ruled, a sprig of marjoram or thyme.

(This doubtless because of the belief that rosemary won't grow unless the wife is paramount!)

Thunder and Lightning

4 tablespoonsful of black treacle	4 tablespoonsful of whipped thick cream

Method. Mix together with 2 tablespoonsful of brown bread crumbs. Add 1 teaspoonful almond essence.

Take off yellow top from a bowl of Devonshire cream and lay it on top. Vanilla can be used, but almond is better.

This can be served on top of a round of sponge cake, if liked.

Miss Eunice Coleman

Miss Eunice Coleman is a Devonian who has spent her whole career in Agriculture. She started teaching in a famous Farm Institute in Cheshire, and then returned to Devon as the County Dairy Husbandry Adviser. She transferred to Bristol as Regional Adviser for the six South West Counties. She has seen modern dairy hygiene develop from farm-house butter and cheesemaking, with small dairy herds, to factory-scale milk production, manufacturing combines, and automation in many production processes. It has proved an absorbing career.

Sandwich Cake

4 oz self-raising flour, sifted
4 oz caster sugar

4 oz butter or margarine
2 standard eggs

Method. Cream fat and sugar together until light and fluffy. Add eggs one at a time, lightly beaten. Beat very well. If mixture curdles at all, beat in a little flour. Fold in remaining flour with a metal spoon. Divide mixture into two 7 in. sandwich tins. Bake in moderate oven, 350°F, gas 4, 15–20 minutes. Cool on wire rack.

Alternatives:

Chocolate. Blend 1 tablespoonful cocoa or chocolate powder with 2 tablespoonsful hot water and allow to cool. After creaming fat and sugar, beat in cooled mixture.

Lemon or Orange. Beat in finely grated rind of 1 lemon or orange to creamed fat and sugar.

Coffee. Add 1 dessertspoonful coffee essence to creamed fat and sugar.

Filling. Sandwich with jam, cream or butter icing.

Butter Icing

2 oz butter
4 oz sieved icing sugar
1 teaspoonful coffee essence, or juice of ½ lemon or orange, or cocoa mixture as above.

Method. Cream together until soft, the 2 oz butter and 4 oz icing sugar, add chosen flavouring, and spread on cake.

❖ ❖ ❖

Traditional Apple Dappy

5 oz flour
Milk to mix
Sugar
1 tablespoon golden syrup

2 oz lard or cooking fat
Diced apples
½ cup water
1 oz margarine

Method. Make pastry, rubbing fat into flour and mixing with cold milk. Roll out and cover with diced apples. Sprinkle generously with sugar. Roll up like a Swiss Roll, cut into slices and lay in a flat baking dish. Pour over these the warm melted syrup, fat and water. Bake approximately 30 minutes, 350°F, gas 4.

Mrs G. K. T. Conn

Exeter.

Mrs Conn's husband is Professor of Physics, University of Exeter.

Angelica Cake

Topping:

1 white of egg	3 oz ground almonds
4 oz caster sugar	1 oz flaked almonds

Cake:

4 oz sugar	5 oz flour
4 oz butter	1½ oz ground almonds
2 eggs and 1 yolk	4 oz currants
4 oz sultanas	4 oz angelica, washed in warm
7 or 7½ in cake tin	water to soften and then
Empty biscuit tin	chopped

Method. Make the topping first. Half-whip the white of egg and fold in the sugar and ground almonds. Put aside until the cake is mixed.

Method. Cream butter and sugar. Add beaten eggs and flour and ground almonds alternately, beating well. Fold in fruit and angelica. Turn into tin, lined with buttered paper. Cover with the topping and sprinkle with flaked almonds.

Place tin on a baking sheet and cover with an empty biscuit tin. Bake at 350°F, Gas 4 for 1½ hours, then remove biscuit tin and return the cake to the oven for a further 30 minutes to brown the top.

Mary Davey

Exeter.

Wife of the Reverend Norman Davey, Diocesan Youth Chaplain.

This is a family recipe, well-tested by several generations. The flavour improves with practice, as you adjust it to your liking.

Golden Mayonnaise

1 hard-boiled egg	¼ teaspoonful salt
6 teaspoonsful caster sugar	¼ teaspoonful pepper
½ teaspoonful mustard	Vinegar
1 small tin evaporated milk	

For a smooth mayonnaise, use yolk only; if white and yolk are used the result is not so smooth, but children like it and it is suitable for potato salad and fish hors d'oeuvre.

Method. Chop egg finely. Add sugar and all dry ingredients. Mix well. Add milk and mix well. Add vinegar slowly, stirring all the time; it quickly thickens.

Use the same day, or keep in a refrigerator, preferably for not more than three days.

D. Francis Davies

Exeter.

Mr D. Francis Davies was trained in Europe, and is now teaching at Exeter Technical College, Food Education Department.

A Breakfast Dish

Half a cup rolled oats   Juice of 1 orange
Juice of ½ a lemon

Method. Soak these for 4 hours. Wash, but do not peel, 1 dessert or cooking, hard apple. Grate whole apple on coarse grater, on to oats. Add 1 tablespoonful full cream condensed sweetened milk, stir and serve.

Nuts, fresh or dried fruit and cream can be added.

Baked Gammon

Method. Soak in cold water for 24 hours. Place in clean roasting tin. Bake in oven all night, 180°F or lower.

Serve with barbecued peaches. Slice peaches, place on grilling tray. Sprinkle well with a mixture of brown sugar and dry mustard. Grill until golden brown. To a good brown gravy, add a little Madeira wine. Serve hot, with potato salad on a bed of lettuce.

Almond Meringue cakes

Method. 5 oz egg whites, 2 oz caster sugar, beat together until a peak is formed.

4 oz ground almonds, lightly toasted, 4 oz caster sugar, mixed together and folded into whites. Spoon or pipe, blobs the size of the 'old' penny, on silicone paper. Dry in very cool oven, as for meringue. Use fresh whipped cream, flavoured with coffee, for filling.

Gateaux—*can be made with this mixture.*

Method. Pipe on to two 8 in circles, or into two sandwich tins, dry in oven as for meringue. Have a 7 in round of sponge about ½ in thick, place on one meringue base, and soak sponge well with Cointreau, Curaçao or other liqueur. Place the other nut meringue on top of sponge. Whip ½ pint double cream, flavoured with the liqueur chosen, and grated zest of orange. Cover top and sides and coat with toasted nibbed almonds. Dust top with icing sugar. Cut into 12 portions.

Note: If no silicone paper is available, blend together, equal quantities of lard and cornflour. Grease trays with this mixture. Nothing ever sticks to this.

Cheese and Onion Flan

Flan ring lined with short pastry, half-cooked blind at 425°F, gas 7. Finely dice onions, sufficient to cover base of flan. Sweat the onions in butter. Grated cheese to fill flan.

Method. Beat 3–4 eggs into 1 pint milk. If you prefer, omit ¼ pint milk, and add ¼ pint dry white wine. Place onion on base of half-cooked case. Fill with grated cheese, and pour on egg custard. Bake at 350°F, gas 4 until set. Serve hot or cold. *Chopped cooked ham or mushrooms can be used as well as, or instead of onion.*

Braised rice—for four people.

4 oz Patna rice	1 oz chopped onion
½ pint chicken stock	2 oz butter
Salt	Milled pepper

1. Place 1 oz butter in pan (ovenproof if possible).
2. Add onion.
3. Cook gently without colouring, 2–3 minutes.
4. Add rice—stir until every grain of rice is coated with hot butter.
5. Cook gently without colouring, 2–3 minutes.
6. Add stock to rice (i.e. twice the amount).
7. Season—cover with buttered paper and bring to boil.
8. Place in hot oven for 15 minutes.
9. Remove and immediately place in cool pan.
10. Carefully mix in remaining butter.
11. Correct seasoning. Serve.

❖ ❖ ❖

Herring Cocktail—*better than prawn and much cheaper!*

Roll-mop herrings

Method. Fillet herrings, by first, pinching along backbone with thumb and forefinger, then slitting the herring open underneath, pressing it flat, and lifting the backbone and all large bones in one operation. Roll these filleted herrings, place in oven-proof dish, add little vinegar and water, a few peppercorns, half a bay leaf, and a clove, cover and bake in medium oven for twenty minutes (about 300°F, gas 2). Leave until cold in the liquid.

For cocktail. Diced cucumber, capers, lettuce, gherkins, paprika, Tabasco sauce (hot and peppery), hard-boiled egg, mayonnaise; oil, vinegar and mustard, using twice as much oil as vinegar.

Method. Wash and shred lettuce, and place in individual glasses. Cut herrings into small pieces and place on lettuce. Sprinkle diced unskinned cucumber over. Mix oil and vinegar and a pinch of dry mustard, and sprinkle over cucumber, etc. Leave to macerate. Prepare mayonnaise. Put mayonnaise into a bowl, add a few drops of Tabasco sauce, diced gherkins, a few capers, and spoon this over contents of the glasses. Place a ring of hard-boiled egg in centre, and a trace of paprika over it.

Sally and Tony Davies

Seaton, Devon,
who keep their own bees, send these traditional Devon recipes for honey.

Honey Cup

4 cups water	2 cups orange juice
2 oz sugar	1 cup lemon juice
1 cup grapefruit juice	8 level tablespoonsful honey

It is advisable to warm the honey for measuring and blending. The cup should, naturally, be served cold.

Honey Eggnog

1 teaspoonful honey	1 egg
1 small teacupful milk	1 tablespoonful brandy

A large pinch each ground ginger and cinnamon.

Method. Having separated the white of egg, beat until stiff. Continue to beat this as you add the honey. Mix the other ingredients and beat them well. Fold in the egg white. Serve in long Sundae glasses.

Honey Shortbread

½ lb butter	2 oz sugar
2 oz honey	14 oz flour

More flour if necessary but try to avoid using more.

Method. Cream butter and sugar, add honey. Work in flour gradually until a stiff dough is obtained. Cut into shapes and bake in a very slow oven, 280°F, gas 1, for 35 minutes.

Honey Fruit Drops

Method. Cream together 1 cup butter and ½ cup honey, add 1 egg and beat well. Add 1 cup chopped dates, 2 cups flour, pinch of salt, 1 cup seedless raisins, ½ teaspoonful cinnamon and ⅔ cup chopped walnuts. Drop in teaspoonsful on greased patty pans. Cook 15 minutes at 325°F, gas 3. Makes 36.

Honey Rolls

Method. Cream together 1 tablespoonful butter and 1½ tablespoonsful honey, add 1 egg and beat well. Add ⅓ cup milk then 2 teacupsful S.R. flour and pinch of salt.

Roll out to ½ in thick, cut with tumbler, fold over to form semi-circle. Bake at 400°F, gas 6, on a greased tray for 12–15 minutes.

With all honey cooking it is preferable if the honey is clear. Any honey can be made clear by holding it at a temperature of 100°F for 2 or 3 hours in a saucepan of water. Avoid using 'warm' honey as its viscosity gets lower as the temperature rises and this can ruin many receipes.

Eric R. Delderfield

Exmouth.

Mr Delderfield is well known for his writing about the West Country. He has thirty-six books to his credit, which vary from Ancient Churches and Inn signs, to West Country Houses, and also is well known for his appearances on Television.

Hedgehog Cake

7 oz unsalted butter	4 egg yolks
4½ oz sugar	Strong black coffee or essence
Packet Boudoir sponge fingers	Few almonds

Method. 1. Cream the butter, mix in the egg yolks and sugar, and carefully add the coffee a little at the time, using sufficient to flavour the creamed mixture.

2. Lay 6 or 8 sponge fingers side by side on a flat dish or board, sprinkle coffee over them, cover with a layer of butter cream, and top with a layer of sponge fingers placed at right angles to the bottom layer. Sprinkle with coffee and cover with creamed mixture.

3. Repeat once again, then cover the outside all round with the coffee cream.

4. Into the outside stick pieces of almond cut into little spikes. Carefully transfer to serving dish.

N.B. This cake is improved if left standing for a day, to allow the coffee to soak in evenly.

———✤·✤·✤———

Many Devonshire housewives, apart from farmers' wives, regularly make clotted cream from the daily pint of milk. One way is to lift the cream from the top of the bottles, with a slender spoon, into a basin, do this for several days, keeping it in the refrigerator until there is enough to make into cream; it can then be put into a stainless steel or suitable saucepan, and over one hour very slowly be brought to just below boiling point, when the top should be wrinkled in appearance. It must not boil. Carefully remove the pan from the stove, leave overnight, and remove the cream next day.

Another method—put 2 or 3 pints of milk into a bowl, and leave in a cool place for a few hours to allow the cream to rise. If the milk is direct from the cow, it should be strained into a bowl.

When milk is ready to scald, place the bowl over a partly-filled pan of hot water, and place on the stove. Bring the water to boiling point so that the temperature of the milk is raised to 165°–170°F winter, 180°F summer, taking 30–35 minutes, and hold at that temperature for 10 minutes. The cream on the top of the milk should then have the characteristic wrinkled appearance. Never allow the milk to boil.

Remove the bowl from the pan of hot water and put in a cool place or refrigerator until the cream head is firm.

Take a sharp knife to free the cream from the sides of the bowl, remove and drain the cream with a skimmer or fish slice to a dish.

Her Grace the Dowager Duchess of Devonshire

Chancellor of the University of Exeter.

'I'm afraid it has no history behind it, but it is a pudding that my family has always liked, and I hope that it may prove popular in your book.'

A favourite pudding

Make a rich custard with 1 pint milk, 2 eggs, 2 extra yolks, sugar, vanilla. Bake, standing in another pan of water, in a fairly slow oven, until gently set. When cold, cover with either strawberry jam, or strawberry ice, or fresh strawberries, then whipped cream, and grated chocolate on top.

———— ❖ ❖ ❖ ————

> Soon as the grey of morning streaks the skies,
> And in the doubtful day the Wood Cock flies,
> Her cleanly pail the pretty housewife bears,
> And singing to the distant field repairs;
> And when the plains with evening dew are spread,
> The milky burthen smokes upon her head.

JOHN GAY, 1685–1732.
Born in Barnstaple.

Mr and Mrs David Dimbleby

Recipe from Josceline Dimbleby, keen cook and photographer, wife of David Dimbleby, broadcaster. Family often visits Devon, and they have holidays on the River Dart.

Dittisham Casserole

A delicious cheap, simple dish, easy to make, and can of course be prepared in the morning, and cooked later. It is best to use fresh 'Scrumpy'. This is the strong dry cider obtainable on draught in most Devon pubs. It has a clean taste similar to dry white wine.

2 lb lean stewing pork or fillet of pork
   cut into chunks
4 oz mushrooms
Coriander seed (should be obtainable
   from good grocers), or Dill seed
Juice ½ lemon

2 onions
1 red or green pimento
Rosemary, fresh if possible
1 large wine glass 'Scrumpy'
   (approx. 1 cup)
Salt and black pepper

Method. Fry pork and sliced onions briefly, just to brown them. Put into casserole dish with sliced pimento and mushrooms. Add the rosemary, coriander, salt and pepper. Pour in 'Scrumpy' and lemon juice.

The meat should be three-quarters covered with juice. If the 'Scrumpy' and lemon juice are not enough, add some light stock or water.

Cover and put in high oven (gas 7–8) for fifteen minutes, and then turn down low (gas mark 2) for 1½–2 hours (425°F, reducing to 300°F). Serves 4–6.

Brigadier H. D. Drew

Exeter.

This was the recipe of my grandmother, married in 1860. She was Mrs Henry Drew of Peamore Cottage, Alphington, near Exeter. She was asked to contribute a Devonshire recipe to a last-century cookery book being compiled in Australia, and this was the one she contributed.

Devonshire Junket

1 quart new milk
Demerara sugar
Grated nutmeg and clotted cream

1½ tablespoonsful prepared rennet
Brandy

Method. Make the milk blood-warm, and place it in a china bowl, into which you have already put three tablespoonsful of brandy, and about 1½ oz of Demerara sugar and some powdered nutmeg. Stir together and complete the flavouring to taste. Stir in 1½ tablespoonsful of essence of rennet and leave in a cool place to set undisturbed. When set, place scalded cream on the curd. This crust of cream should if possible completely cover the curd. Cover with a thick sprinkling of Demerara sugar and grated nutmeg and pour 2 tablespoonsful of brandy over the whole.

Barbara Dunhill

Lydford, Okehampton.

Mrs Dunhill, a part-time Devonian though an enthusiastic one. Married to David Dunhill, a radio announcer and newsreader with the B.B.C.

Four children—two married daughters and twin sons of seventeen—and thus has done a lot of cooking.

Enjoys adapting and inventing recipes.

Had professional training in the visual arts and considers this highly relevant to the running of her home and family.

Fish Pie

The Fish:

1½ lb fillet of cod (or haddock, rockfish, etc. or a mixture of fish)
About one-third pint dry cider, or cider and water

Method. Skin the fish and cut into 1–1½ inch pieces. Put these into a fireproof dish, seasoning as you go. Add the cider, cover the dish and put into the oven (Reg. 6 or 400°F). Cook for about 15 minutes. Pour off the liquor, use for sauce.

The Sauce:

1 medium sized onion, chopped small
¼ lb mushrooms, halved, or cut even smaller according to size
1 teaspoonful, or more, of sugar
2 rashers of bacon cut into strips
1 small tin tomatoes, the juice and flesh sieved
Chopped parsley

Method. Cook the onion in a knob of butter or margarine in a saucepan until it is soft but not brown.

Add the bacon and stir it about till the fat is melted. Now stir in a good tablespoonful of flour.

Add liquor from the fish and the sieved tomatoes until you have rather a thick sauce.

Add the mushrooms, the sugar and, perhaps, more seasoning and the parsley if you have it.

Pour this over the fish stirring gently so as not to break it up. Cover the dish with a pastry crust, with mashed potato or with coarsely grated breadcrumbs. Dot the last two with butter and put the dish into the oven to cook and brown.

Instead of mushrooms and bacon, shrimps, prawns or mussels could be used.

33

Annette Dunsford

Claims that she has been a pretty average housewife, who has never liked house-work, is a grandmother, and O.A.P. Interested in many things, she sits on com-mittees, but is annoyed when her family calls her a 'committee woman'!

Mother-in-Law's Potato Cake

To be eaten hot out of the oven for tea, particularly good if you haven't had lunch.

8 oz self-raising flour	4 oz mixed fruit and peel
4 oz margarine and beef dripping	½ teaspoon mixed spice
4 oz brown sugar	1 egg (no other moisture)
8 oz mashed potatoes	Pinch salt

Method. Rub the fat into the flour, mix in all the dry ingredients, bind with the beaten egg. Put in a greased flat tin 7 in. by 7 in. Bake about 1¼ hours. Gas 5, 375°F.

Ann Elliot

Topsham, Devon.

Ann Elliot is a Devonian, born in Tavistock. Her husband, Dr David Hawksley Elliot—British—led the American expedition to the Antarctic in the autumn of 1969, and found the famous fossils on the Coalsack Bluff which an American Polar Science statesman has described as 'one of the truly great fossil finds of all time'.

Geologists consider that this proves that Antarctica was connected, probably for at least 60 million years, to Africa, South America, India and Australia.

Lemon Chicken

One can prepare this early in the day to prevent last minute 'flaps'.
Ingredients—for six helpings:

6 pieces chicken	½ teaspoonful paprika
1 teaspoonful salt	1 tablespoonful flour
2 lemons	Oil for frying
2 tablespoonsful brown sugar	1 cup chicken stock or 1 chicken
Sprig of fresh mint (optional but	stock cube and 1 cup water
delicious if it's in season)	

Method. Wash and dry chicken. Grate rind of 1 lemon. Cut it in half and rub the chicken with cut surfaces. Shake chicken in paper bag with flour, salt and paprika. Brown chicken in oil in frying pan and transfer to casserole in layers interspersed with brown sugar, the grated rind and the second lemon cut in very thin slices. Pour over the stock, add mint on top and cover. Cook at 350°F, or Regulo 4 for 1 hour and serve with baked potatoes and a green salad.

Lemon Sponge

1 oz gelatine	¾ lb lump sugar
Juice and grated rind of 2 lemons	1 pint water
2 egg whites	

Method. Put all but egg whites into a saucepan and stir till it just boils. Cool. Beat egg whites till stiff then beat all together to a stiff froth.

Mrs W. Elliot Batt

Topsham.

Chicken Casserole—for 4.

chicken
or 2 onions
cooking apple
level teaspoonful brown sugar
Salt and pepper to taste

½ lb mushrooms
Medium tin tomatoes
1 teaspoonful mild mustard
1 tin new potatoes

Method. 1. Warm and grease deep casserole dish. At bottom place potatoes, sliced or whole. 2. Cover with finely sliced apple. 3. Fry finely sliced onions until brown. 4. Add to pan, tomatoes, mustard, sugar and seasoning. 5. Place contents of pan in casserole and cook for about 20 minutes in low oven. 6. Meanwhile, joint chicken and brown in pan with butter and oil. Remove casserole from oven, place chicken joints on top of the vegetables and return to oven for 30–40 minutes.

P. M. Evans

Chudleigh, South Devon.

Dutch Pudding

egg
teaspoonful vanilla essence
cup plain flour
teaspoonful salt
cup nut meats, or chopped nuts

¾ cup of caster sugar
(don't stint)
1¼ teaspoonsful baking powder
1 cup diced sour apples
¼ teaspoonful cinnamon.

Method. Beat egg until pale and thick. Slowly add sugar and vanilla and beat well. Sift flour, B.P. and salt and add to sugar and egg. Add diced apples, nuts and cinnamon. Pour into a 10 in. Pyrex dish. The higher the sides the better. Bake 45 minutes at 325°F, Reg. 3. Serve warm with whipped or poured cream.

Dutch origin, by way of Topsham.

————✦·✦·✦————

Shell House, Topsham, on the Strand, was built at the end of the sixteenth century; it contains a fine example of a Grinling Gibbons ceiling, suspended by chains. A huge shell, moulded in plaster, decorates the lintel above the front door, probably being a unique sign or password that this house contained a priest's hole or hiding place. . . . Many other houses of the sixteenth and seventeenth centuries, rich in historical interest, are found along the Strand, where the wealthy Elizabethan merchants built their homes. Little gardens, facing across the road, were once the landing places for cargo ships in the days when Topsham was the principal port in the Exe estuary.

Prince Orange House, built on the Strand in 1688, may have been the repository for some of William of Orange's possessions, which were brought by sea from Brixham to Topsham when he landed in Devonshire during that year.

Kay M. Ewell

Y.W.C.A. West Field Secretary

'*I have worked with the Y.W.C.A. as a Youth Leader, Club Leader and General Secretary in Berkshire, Surrey, London and New Zealand, before coming to the West Country, where I have stayed longer than anywhere else.*'

Baked Savoury Herrings (to be eaten hot or cold).

2 lb herrings (or 1 lb herring fillets)
2 tablespoonsful rolled oats, oatmeal or breadcrumbs

1 small onion, finely chopped
1 level teaspoonful mixed herbs (3 tablespoonsful packet stuffing could be used instead)

Salt, pepper, oil or softened butter or margarine, a little lemon juice or cider vinegar to soften any bones.

Method. Fillet herrings, sprinkle them with finely chopped onion, salt, pepper, mixed herbs and half of the rolled oats. Roll up, and place in greased baking tin or fireproof dish, brush with oil or fat, sprinkle with rolled oats.

Bake near the top of oven (400°F, gas 6), for 20 minutes. Serve hot or cold.

Soft herring roes, dipped in oatmeal, and fried, make a cocktail savoury.

Toffee Apples for Fairings

3 lb sugar
1 tablespoonful vinegar
12 oz water (1½ breakfast cups)

1 teaspoonful cream of tartar
1 tablespoonful golden syrup

Method. Put all in a saucepan. Heat slowly and stir until quite dissolved. Bring to boil. Put lid on saucepan for one minute until steam puffs out. Continue boiling. To test, take a wooden stick and a cup of cold water. Dip stick in water, then in toffee, then in water again. If toffee is brittle, take off stove, wait until bubbling ceases then dip apples. This will do about 40 apples.

Cream Cheese Walnuts

4 oz cream cheese, beaten with 2–3 teaspoonsful cream, and 2 teaspoonsful caster sugar. Roll this round walnut halves. At once roll in chopped parsley. The parsley will not cling if the outside is the least bit dry.

---- ❖ ❖ ❖ ----

Rum Butter to serve with Christmas Pudding.

8 oz moist brown sugar and rum to taste   8 oz butter

Method. Melt butter over low heat, gradually add sugar, beating all the time, finally add rum. Serve with Devonshire cream as well.

This is delicious spread over thin slices of Christmas pudding, with cream on top.

Exmouth Y.W.C.A.

Miss Helen Christie, Exmouth.

Flaming Punch

6 tablespoonsful honey
1 tin sliced pineapple

1 bottle white wine
½ pint rum

Method. Place honey in flameproof dish, or punch bowl, add sliced pineapple. Heat white wine until it is just on boiling point, then pour it on honey and pineapple, and mix well until honey is melted. Heat rum till boiling point, pour very gently on top of honey, pineapple and wine. Put a light to the mixture, which will readily flame. *'This is an ideal Christmas drink.'*

———✧–✧–✧———

Mrs Lott, Woodbury, near Exeter.

Two old Devonshire recipes.

Devon Fish Pie

1¼ lb cooked potatoes, ½ lb cooked fish, 1 hard-boiled egg, ½ pint white sauce (1 oz butter, 1 oz flour, blend over gentle heat, gradually add ¼ pint cold milk and ½ pint cold fish stock or water.

Method. If the liquids are hot, blend butter and flour and remove pan from heat to add the liquids, then boil. Add a pinch cayenne pepper, and salt.

Butter a pie-dish, and put in layers of potatoes, fish, sauce, and sliced egg, leaving plenty of potatoes for top. Brush with a little milk or egg, and bake in a moderate oven until lightly browned. 350°F, gas 4.

Elderflower Sparkling Wine

2 heads elderflower in full bloom
1 lemon
2 tablespoons white vinegar

1 gallon cold water
1½ lb loaf sugar

Method. Squeeze the juice out of the lemon. Cut the rind in four, and put this with the flowers, sugar and vinegar in a large jug. Pour in the cold water and leave to steep for 24 hours. Strain off and bottle in screw-topped bottles and keep for two weeks at least, before using.

This is a delicious sparkling drink.

Miss Agatha Farrell

House Manager, Thomas Hall, Exeter University, Hall of Residence for Women.

Devonshire Drops

8 oz sieved flour   2½ oz sieved icing sugar
8 oz butter

Method. Cream butter, gradually cream in sugar and flour, keeping the mixture very soft. Pipe out on a slightly greased tin with a savoy star tube, in rounds. Let them stand two hours before baking. Bake 20–30 minutes in a slow oven till pale brown. 275–300°F, gas 1–2.

These will keep in an airtight tin. Fill with jam and sprinkle with icing sugar before eating them.

Petronel Ferens

Ipplepen, near Newton Abbot.

Jugged Beef for four people.

1¾ lb chuck (stewing) beef   2 oz seasoned flour
Oil or fat for frying   2 small onions stuck with 4 cloves
Grated rind of ½ lemon   each
Bouquet garni   6 small mushrooms
¾ pint bouillon

Method. Cut meat into three-inch pieces, discarding fat and skin. Roll in seasoned flour. Heat oil or fat in frying pan, fry meat lightly, just to brown.

Transfer to casserole, add onion, lemon rind, bouquet garni, mushrooms and bouillon. Cover tightly and cook *slowly* for at least 3 hours. Remove bouquet garni and onions before serving.

This really tastes like a less rich jugged hare; a little red wine can be added if desired.

I find it most useful to put in the oven before a long morning's shopping if one brings someone home to lunch.

Cheese Sables—*These are most appetising and I generally make double the quantity.*

3 oz plain flour   Salt and cayenne pepper
3 oz butter   3 oz grated cheese (including some
1 beaten egg   parmesan if possible)

Method. Sift flour with salt and pepper (small pinch) into a mixing bowl; add butter cut into small pieces. Rub butter into flour, then add cheese and press together into a paste. Roll out fairly thinly and cut into rounds or two inch strips, as preferred. Brush with beaten egg. Bake in a moderate oven (375°F or Reg. 5) to a good golden brown (ten minutes or less).

Mrs M. B. Ford

Copplestone, Devon.

I have been connected with agriculture most of my life having lived in the area of the lovely red Devon soil around Crediton and Copplestone, areas of delightful scenery. I am one of the founder members of the Copplestone Women's Institute, a happy group of which I am at present President. Our village has numerous other activities enabling us all to take part in its life.

Chocolate Steamed Cake

5 oz self-raising flour	1 oz margarine
2 oz caster sugar	1 tablespoonful syrup
1 saltspoonful bi-carbonate of soda	3 dessertspoonsful cocoa
Enough milk to make a batter	

Method. Mix together the sugar, flour and cocoa. Rub in the margarine. Warm the syrup and add it with the bi-carbonate of soda dissolved in a little milk, and enough milk to make a thick batter. Pour the mixture into a 7 in. cake tin, cover the top with a piece of grease proof paper and steam for one hour. Let it stand for two minutes before turning out.

Leave on cake stand until cold. Cut in half, fill with cream. Cover the top of the cake with chocolate icing. Three tablespoonsful icing sugar, 2 dessertspoonsful cocoa and a little warm water. Spread evenly on top.

We are indebted to Messrs McDougalls' Cookery Service for the following information.

Different types of flour

A. Self-raising. This is suitable for general household use. Many housewives use it for all their home baking.

B. Plain flour. Basically similar to A, but without the raising ingredients. It can therefore be used in recipes for which raising ingredients are not essential, e.g., sauces, pancakes, short pastries, whisked sponges, etc. This type of flour is good for rich yeast recipes—e.g. chelsea buns, tea breads etc.

C. Strong plain flour. Specially milled for home breadmaking. It is also excellent for Yorkshire Pudding and rich pastries (flaky, rough puff and puff).

D. Wholemeal flour. Must contain 100% of the cleaned whole wheat grains.

E. Wheatmeal flour. Some of the coarsest bran is removed, usually 85%–95%.

Extraction rate means the percentage of the whole grain that remains in the flour after milling,

> e.g. Wholemeal flour is 100%
> White flour is 70%-72%

The Lady Margaret Fortescue

Barnstaple.

Summer Dinner Party Menu—for eight people.

Oyster Vol-au-Vent

1 cooked vol-au-vent case (keep warm)   1¼ pints rich white sauce
8 oysters (prepared) or 4 cans oysters (large size)
Make this sauce from the oyster juices, cream, white wine and a pinch of
nutmeg.

Method. If oysters are large, slice to suit one's taste, gently put the oysters
into the prepared sauce, make very hot (but not to boil). When ready fill
vol-au-vent case, serve at once. *Suggested wine:* Steinwein.

Cold Fillet of Beef

Two 2½ lb fillets of beef (trimmed)   Seasoning
Larding pieces   Tin pâté de foie gras
Aspic jelly   Mushrooms, marinaded in French
                                      dressing

Method. Season and lard fillets, cook to 'underdone', when cold remove
fat, etc. cover with a good aspic jelly—when set slice in rounds about ¾ in.
thickness, put a little round of Pâté, about the size of a shilling, on the centre
of each piece; arrange on centre of silver dish with chopped aspic down one
side and the dark side of mushrooms down the other. Serve with sauté
potatoes, ratatouille and tossed green salad. *Suggested wine:* Volnay.

Melon and Ginger Ice
Melon Water Ice

4½ oz caster sugar   1 pint of water
2 lemons   1 glass of maraschino syrup
1½ ripe melons

Method. Peel the melons, pound flesh until smooth, strain juice, dissolve
the caster sugar in the water—when cold add to melon juice, with the
juices of the lemons and maraschino syrup. This is particularly good if
champagne is used instead of water. Freeze.

Ginger Ice Cream

3 oz. preserved ginger   3 tablespoons of maraschino
1½ pints cream   syrup
6 egg yolks   3 oz caster sugar

Method. Mince and pound preserved ginger with the syrup, then add the
cream, eggs and sugar—stir this mixture altogether over the heat until
nicely thickened, allow to cool. Freeze. When almost frozen put the above
mixtures in a soufflé dish with a band of paper around the top—fill one side
with Melon Water Ice and the other with Ginger Ice Cream—return to ice
box until wanted. Decorate with strips of preserved ginger and whipped
cream. Remove paper band. Serve with Petit Fours.
  Suggested wine: Château Pajot (Enclave Yquem).

Mrs Thomas Fox

Chairman, Y.W.C.A. West Council.

Three family favourites (each suggested by a different member of the family).

Chicken and Rice

One boiled fowl or cooked chicken, *size according to number to feed. (If a spring chicken, joints can be fried first in same pan as the rest.)*

2 oz per person 'golden Italian' or Patna long rice	8 oz mushrooms
2–4 oz cashew nuts	2 firm cooking apples
2 oz sultanas	1 large onion
1 green pepper (optional)	1 head celery

Method. Cook and joint the chicken. (If a fowl, the outer celery can be cooked with it.) Melt 4 oz butter or margarine, or 3 tablespoons olive oil, or a mixture of both, in a pan big enough to take all ingredients. Fry the rice in this, then drain it, and put it in boiling salted water until just tender, but not squashy. Drain it well. Run a little cold water on it to separate the grains and shake and drain again, and keep it in a cloth.

Slice onion and green pepper in fine rings and cook in the oil, until clear and tender, not brown. Chop celery, mushrooms if large, and apple, to sultana-size. Toss all in the fat with the sultanas. Season well with ground pepper, salt, and add chicken joints and rice. Turn all over till well-coated and mixed. Or chicken can be served around piled rice mixture. Serve piping hot.

This can all be cooked beforehand, and kept hot if well-covered. Mix just before serving.

Date Cake

A war-time recipe which my grandmother always had baked in a ring-mould. We do the same, since I found one in a sale at an old house. It needs a brush to grease it properly.

12 oz flour	6 oz butter or margarine
6 oz brown sugar	4–8 oz dates, the more the better
1 teaspoonful mixed spice	1 teaspoonful bi-carbonate of soda
1 teaspoonful vinegar	½ teaspoonful salt
½ pint milk (approx.)	

Method. Rub fat into flour, add the dry ingredients. Chop dates, mix the soda with a little of the milk, and add to the dry ingredients. Add lastly the vinegar and milk to mix to a fairly soft consistency. Put in a greased tin and bake in a moderate oven 2 hours.

This cake will keep for several weeks and improves if not cut for at least a week. Good for 'pack lunches'.

Beef Olives

Very good to 'come home to', if you have a solid fuel cooker, or simmering ring with well-sealed hot-pot.

Braising steak, 3–4 oz per person. Ask the butcher to cut into thin slices, or they can be beaten thin. Chuck or shin will do.

8 oz white breadcrumbs	1 bay leaf, or bouquet garni
1 onion, 1 oz parsley, 1 leaf of sage (all chopped fine)	1 egg Seasoned flour

Method. Make a forcemeat of crumbs, parsley, onion, sage, egg, pepper and salt to taste. Trim beef into pieces about 2 in. by 4 in. leaving some fat on. Roll each round a spoonful of stuffing and tie or skewer. Roll in seasoned flour and put into casserole. Cover and heat quickly, adding a teaspoonful of dripping if there is no beef fat. Let the meat brown, turning if necessary; sprinkle with flour to take up the fat, add 2 oz mushrooms if liked, but not necessary, the bay leaf or bouquet garni, and cover with cold water. Put on the lid, with greaseproof or foil if it is not a good fit, and simmer for 2 hours, or longer if stewing beef is used. Before serving, remove string or skewers and bouquet garni or bay leaf. Served with creamed potatoes and baked tomatoes or some green vegetables.

Mrs A. T. J. Graham

Bowhay Farm, Aish, Near Totnes.

County Commissioner-designate, Girl Guides.

Most people probably expect a camp cookery recipe from a Guide. I have not camped for many years but I do spend a lot of time sailing, hate cooking at sea and therefore like to prepare in advance meals which can take care of themselves and provide a good hot meal after several hours of non-attention. You will also find this useful at home, when you want to talk to your friends without culinary interruptions. The following beef recipe provides an interesting main course, and in this part of Devon a light pâté of smoked mackerel would be appropriate to precede it, and to follow it an open tart or flan of apples.

Pate of Smoked Mackerel—for 4 people.

8 oz smoked mackerel, pounded with 8 oz unsalted butter and lemon juice and cream added according to taste. Serve with thin brown bread and butter.

Beef in the manner of Aish (or Boeuf a la Bowhay)

Method. Choose a good thick chunk of beef, such as topside, weighing about 4 pounds and neatly tied in an oblong shape. Brown the meat on all sides in olive oil or butter, or a mixture of both, using a strong pan with a well-fitting lid, and which can go in the oven. During the browning process, add some 3 oz of chopped salt pork or 'green' bacon. Now put in three or four shallots (or a large onion, cut up), a crushed clove of garlic, 3 or 4 cut-up tomatoes, 2 carrots, a small handful of coarsely chopped olives, a good bunch of herbs including bay leaf and rosemary, salt and freshly-ground pepper. Pour in a good tumbler of red wine, at least a tablespoonful of brandy, set alight. Cover with a sheet of foil and the lid, and cook in the lowest possible oven for 7 or 8 hours. *It will cook almost imperceptibly and emerge deliciously tender, though not 'falling abroad', to use a favourite Devonian expression.*

The ingredients can be varied according to what you have to hand. Rum or whisky instead of brandy for example, and cider or beer instead of wine. Two pigs trotters can be included in the cooking, plus a little more liquid. This will enrich the sauce and produce a good jelly if the dish is eaten cold. The best accompaniment is plain boiled rice or mashed potato which will help to absorb any excess fat from the sauce. Arrange the meat in fairly thick slices in a border of rice or potato with the sauce poured over.

Apple Tart or Flan

Prepare pastry several hours ahead if possible.

Make pastry according to Mr Sutherland's recipe for Galette Montmorency; quantities are enough for two 9 in. flans. If making in a dish, put wide strips of foil under the pastry, to make it easy to lift out the cooked flan.

Cover the pastry with sliced cooking apples, and pour thick custard sauce over.

Method. Bake 380°F–400°F, gas 5–6, 30 minutes. Leave for 2 minutes, then lift carefully on to wire tray, or put on tray and lift flan ring at once.

Custard Sauce

1 pint milk
2 oz sugar
2 eggs

1 tablespoonful arrowroot,
custard powder or potato flour

Method. Boil milk, beat eggs, sugar and chosen starch in bowl, add gradually a little hot milk, then add all of it. Rinse pan, pour the custard into it, and stir constantly until it just boils. Remove from the heat.

Dried milk makes a creamy custard sauce. Beat 2 or 3 spoonsful with eggs, sugar and chosen starch, blend with a little hot water, pour on the rest of the pint of water, and bring just to the boil, stirring constantly.

If it is not perfectly smooth, whisk, or sieve, or liquidise the custard. The 'starch' saves it from curdling.

❖ ❖ ❖

In 1688, William of Orange, who had landed at Brixham, held his first Parliament in Berry Pomeroy, the neighbouring parish to Aish; the villagers of Aish did not welcome him with open arms, but to prove that they were not hostile, slowly rolled, one by one, apples towards him, from a little distance, presumably while sitting on the fence.

Bridget Grant-Watson

Exeter.

Miss Grant-Watson describes herself as a gardening char, but she is a pruning expert, and a specialist in 'architecturally' shaping trees, as a focal point in a garden. She renovates old gardens. She cares for the gardens of several blind people, including a First-World-War blind veteran; her charges range from Mrs Winter's three rose trees in a tiny garden tucked behind a non-conformist chapel to beautiful gardens open to the public. She gives the following practical recipes.

Westcountry Brack

1 lb dried fruit (raisins, sultanas, currants)
½ lb self-raising flour
1 egg yolk

8 oz dark brown sugar
½ pint strained cold tea
1 egg
Pinch salt

Method. Soak fruit and sugar overnight in the tea. Mix with rest of ingredients. Put in loaf tin. Bake 1¼ hours, 400°F, Gas 6. Slice thinly, spread with butter.

Overnight Biscuits

Method. Mix four cupsful quick-cooking oats, 2 cupsful brown sugar, 1 cup salad oil, leave overnight. Next day, mix in 2 beaten eggs, ½ teaspoonful almond extract, 1 teaspoonful salt. Drop from a teaspoon on to a greased baking sheet. Bake 325°F, Gas 3, for 10–15 minutes. Remove promptly from tin when cooked.

Miss Helen Graveney

Matron of City Hospital, Exeter, until 1970.

Marmalade—*Quick and easy.*

1 lb Seville oranges
1 sweet orange
1 teaspoonful lemon juice

1½ pints water
2 lb granulated sugar (warmed)

Method. Wash oranges, put whole into a pan with the water. Simmer slowly until oranges are soft enough to push a wooden skewer through easily. Remove fruit from the pan, cut into chunky pieces or put through mincer. Save all pips, return these to the liquid in the pan and simmer for 10 minutes. Strain off pips and return liquid to pan, add fruit, sugar and lemon juice.

Stir over gentle heat until sugar dissolves, then boil rapidly, allowing marmalade to rise well into the pan—until setting point is reached (about ¼ hour). Allow to cool, stir, pour into warm jars.

Ginger Sponge Cake. *Is economical, simple to make and keeps well. Can be varied by icing with plain water icing, or butter icing, or add fruit or chopped ginger to mixture.*

6 oz self-raising flour
4 oz syrup or treacle or mixed
1 heaped teaspoonful ginger
1 teacupful milk

2 oz sugar
3 oz fat, lard, margarine or butter
1 level teaspoonful bicarbonate of soda

Method. Rub fat into flour—make well—add sugar and syrup and ginger. Boil milk, add bicarbonate of soda to this. Pour into mixture and mix the batter well. Pour into a well greased tin. Bake in moderate oven for about 1 hour.

Mrs F. E. Griffith-Morgan

J.P. and Warden of Moberly House, University Hall of Residence, Exeter.

Here is a very pleasant concoction and delicious sweet.

The recipe allows six portions:

The whites of 2 large eggs
6 tablespoonsful (level) caster sugar
This constitutes the *base.*

1 teaspoonful cornflour
Lemon juice

6 tinned or poached fresh half pears (medium tin) well drained and one glacé cherry
4 oz whipped cream
This is the *topping.*

Method. Beat up whites. When stiff add 3 tablespoonsful sugar and beat to a meringue consistency. Fold in second 3 tablespoonsful sugar. Fold in cornflour and lemon juice. Line a round 7 in. tin with greased paper bottom and sides. Pour in the mixture. Bake at No. 2 (300–325°F) for ¼ hour and then at No. 1 gas (275°F), for ½ hour. Turn on rack. Use later same day. Spread whipped cream on top, place pears in a circle on the cream with cherry in the centre.

Ann Gundry

Exeter.

Therapeutic Dietician, one-time head of the Dietetic Department, Guy's Hospital and wife of Peter Gundry, F.R.I.B.A., J.P., Surveyor to the Fabric of Exeter Cathedral. This is the most complete and perfect example of the fourteenth century 'decorated' period of Medieval Architecture and provides the longest uninterrupted length of vaulting in the world.

Asparagus Stuffed Sole with Mushroom Sauce

4 large sole (filleted)	¼ pint strained fish stock or water
¼ pint dry white wine	1 bay leaf
6 peppercorns	16 asparagus tips (cooked fresh or
Seasoning	tinned)
Sauce:	
½–¾ pint milk	1 lb mushrooms
2 oz butter	2 oz plain flour
Salt and pepper	Parsley

Method. 1. Place an asparagus tip on each fillet, roll up and put into a fireproof dish.

2. Pour over stock and wine.

3. Add bay leaf, peppercorns and a little salt.

4. Cover and cook for 15–20 minutes at mark 4 (350°F).

5. When cooked, drain off the liquid and make up to 1¼ pints with milk, removing peppercorns and bay leaf.

6. Keep rolled fillets covered, in a very low oven while the sauce is prepared.

7. Slice the mushrooms and add, with their chopped stalks, to the milk and stock.

8. Infuse in a basin over a pan of hot water for 15 minutes, then drain off the liquor, reserving the mushrooms.

9. Make a sauce by cooking together the butter and flour, then gradually adding the liquor, stirring until smooth. Bring to the boil and cook gently for 3–4 minutes.

10. Add the mushrooms, return to the boil and pour over the rolled fillets. Garnish with parsley. Serves 8.

Mrs Barbara Hall

Organising Secretary, Devon Association of Youth Clubs.

Meringue Cake with Devonshire Cream

(Very light pudding—most suitable after large Sunday lunch.)

Method. Beat until stiff, but not dry, three egg whites, pinch salt. Add gradually, 6 oz caster sugar and continue beating until stiff. Sift and fold in, 1 dessertspoonful cornflour, add 2 teaspoonsful vinegar and, if liked, 1 teaspoonful vanilla essence. Bake 1½ to 2 hours, 250°F or Regulo ½.

Important. Line a 7 in. sponge tin as for a cake, with greaseproof paper on sides and bottom. Brush well with oil, place mixture in and smooth over. Serve with Devonshire Cream. Makes four 'reasonable' portions.

Mrs W. J. Hallett

Mayoress of Exeter, 1969–1970.

Strawberry Ice Cream

1 lb good strawberries
7 oz granulated sugar
1 tablespoonful lemon juice
¼ teaspoonful salt

1 teaspoonful gelatine
1 tablespoonful cold water
½ pint, no more, milk
½ pint whipped cream

Pre-set ice box of refrigerator to coldest point.

Method. 1. Sieve the strawberries: measure purée which should be about ¾ pint. Add sugar, lemon juice and salt and stir well. Cover and cool in refrigerator.
2. Meanwhile, soften gelatine in water and make up with milk to ½ pint. Heat very gently (do not boil) to dissolve gelatine.
3. Cool and add to purée, then fold in whipped cream, that is, do not beat, but gently amalgamate them.
4. Turn into freezing dish and place in ice box of refrigerator. When firm, store as ordinary ice block, at about No. 4 setting.

———— ❖ ❖ ❖ ————

'What is the secret of the thatcher's art? How comes about his finished product, a beautiful roof so pleasing to the eye? How even does he start, turn the corners, or finish leaving no visible joins?

'Well! It's just like slating a roof, starting at the eaves and finishing at the ridge, but the materials are straws or reeds and the nails are wooden spears.

'The craftsmanship is ability to handle the material, which skill is only acquired with years of practice. The art is in the hand and eye working together.

'The thatcher needs very busy hands and fingers, for nothing is happening if they are still.

'His enemies are wind and sun. Light straws blow easily or slip and slide when shiny dry like metal rods. This is why the thatcher wets his reed, and keeps it well pinned down, or he could be surrounded soon by a heap of litter.

'You yourself if stranded on a desert island and needing shelter, would solve the mystery of thatching. Your first attempt with leaves or rushes would look like an inverted rooks' nest, but you would be dry and with practice you would achieve a work of art.'

H. N. SNOWDON.

Wendy Hannam

Wife of John Hannam, Exeter's Member of Parliament.

'*I hope my recipe will be found to be palatable. I love cooking but am finding already that as the wife of a Member of Parliament it is increasingly difficult to spend as much time as I would like in preparing those special meals which we wives sometimes like to produce for the outstanding occasion.*

'*Soup is a very useful stand-by to reinforce the light snacks upon which we seem to live recently.*

'*In addition to travelling to and fro between our home in Chiselborough and Westminster and acting as a chauffeur for my husband, I am busily occupied at the moment in trying to furnish a small flat we have taken near the House. I am doing it by accumulating bits and pieces as we go along.*

'*My husband and I appreciate the invaluable contribution made by the voluntary organisations such as the Y.W.C.A., for the benefit of the community and we both wish your Association well.*'

Chilled Cauliflower Soup

Method. Put one cauliflower in a saucepan with one onion cut in half and a bay leaf.

Cover with milk and cook gently until soft.

Remove bay leaf and place in liquidiser together with a dessertspoonful of curry powder, salt and pepper to taste.

After liquidising, pour through fine sieve into bowl.

Place in fridge when cool, and leave until needed. Serve in individual soup bowls, add cream and chopped chives or parsley, to decorate.

Mrs M. F. Hawthorn

Topsham.

'*I heard this recipe when I was dressing for breakfast, in my little hotel room, from the B.B.C. London, during the war. I wrote it down, as doing so made the time when I could have a home again, seem nearer. It is a reliable recipe. I have used it for many years.*'

Sponge Cake

4 oz flour	1 oz fat
2 oz sugar	1 level tablespoonful golden syrup
1 egg	2 level teaspoonsful baking powder
Good ½ teacup milk, or milk and water	½ teaspoonful bi-carbonate of soda

Method. Cream fat and sugar and syrup as well as possible. Add sifted flour and baking powder alternately with well-beaten egg to creamed mixture. Dissolve bi-carbonate of soda in milk and add to mixture. Beat thoroughly. Put into greased and floured sandwich tins, and bake in hot oven, Reg. 6 or 7, gas, 400°F to 425°F.

N.B. A nicer chocolate cake can be made by removing 1 tablespoonful flour, and replacing it with cocoa, 1 tablespoonful. I usually cream some margarine, sugar and cocoa to make a filling for the cake.

Mrs Michael Heseltine

Wife of the Member of Parliament for Tavistock.
Holbeton, South Devon.

We find the mussels for this soup on the shores of the Erme estuary where we live. We pick them up at low tide, where the river meets the open sea, but the biggest and best are found in a deep pool up the estuary, and have to be dived for in snorkel and flippers. They are worth the effort.

Mussel Soup

Method. Collect 1 quart of fresh mussels at low tide. Cover with fresh water and discard any which are already open. Scrub under cold running water and scrape off beards. Then leave under running tap for a further 10 minutes.

Place in a heavy pan with 6 whole peppercorns, chopped parsley, thyme, chives, bay leaf and mace, 1 tablespoonful of butter and a gill of white wine. Cover and bring to the boil shaking frequently. After five minutes the shells will open—any that persist in remaining closed should be rejected. Remove mussels, stir in ¾ oz flour until smooth. Add 1½ pints of good fish stock, season, bring to boil, and simmer for 5 minutes. Return mussels to pan and simmer again for 5 minutes. Thicken soup with one gill of double cream and 2 egg yolks beaten together. Serve with triangular croutons and chopped parsley.

Mrs P. S. Heyward

Artist,
Clyst St. George, Near Exeter.

Spanish Cream

1½ pints milk	¾ oz gelatine
3 eggs, separated, whites stiffly whipped	½ teacupful caster sugar

Flavouring—vanilla, wine, lemon, brandy or liqueur

Method. Soak gelatine in a cup of warm milk. Put rest of milk on to boil. When boiling pour on to well-beaten egg yolks and sugar. Return to rinsed pan and stir until it boils. Add flavouring and pour on to stiffly whipped whites of eggs, adding melted gelatine and milk. Pour into a wet mould and when set, turn out. The custard must boil or it will separate. The top of the Spanish Cream should be clear amber, and the custard below, forming two distinct layers.

N.B. The custard should only just boil—do not keep it cooking.

———✧–✧–✧———

Edible gelatine is pure protein and is consequently susceptible to heat and attack from bacteria, which cause breakdown of the structure. Since jelly strength and viscosity are the most important properties of gelatine, it is inadvisable to subject gelatine solution to boiling temperatures, as this will lower the strength and viscosity and therefore, the setting power of gelatine.

Mary Higgins

Combe-in-Teignhead.

Devon County Chairman of the Women's Institute from 1967–1970.

Bread Rolls

1 lb plain flour
1 teaspoonful salt
1 oz lard

1 oz yeast
1 teaspoonful sugar
½ pint milk

Method. Sieve and mix together flour and salt. Rub in lard very finely. Cream yeast with sugar until liquid, add lukewarm milk. Make a well in centre of flour and pour in liquid. Mix well. Turn out on to a floured board and knead well, working from sides to middle, until dough becomes smooth and pliable and leaves the hands clean. Put dough into a bowl, cover with a damp cloth, and put in a warm place to rise until double its bulk. Take from bowl, turn on to a floured board, and knead gently. Shape into small balls or fingers and put on a greased baking sheet. Put to rise again in a warm place. When well risen and light, bake in a hot oven for 15–20 minutes, 450°F, Gas 8.

These rolls keep well in a deep freezer.

Curry Cream Sauce

2 tablespoonsful oil
1 tablespoonful chopped onion
1 clove garlic
1 dessertspoonful curry powder
½ pint mayonnaise (see Lady Caradon's recipe)

1 teaspoonful tomato purée
Scant ¼ pint strong tomato juice
2–3 slices lemon
1 good tablespoonful apricot jam

Method. Soften onion in the oil with chopped garlic. Add curry powder, and cook for a few minutes, then add the purée and tomato juice. Simmer 10–12 minutes, adding seasoning and the lemon. Stir in the jam until dissolved and strain. Cool slightly, add to the mayonnaise and adjust seasoning.

This is an excellent sauce for using with cold shredded chicken or hard-boiled eggs or with cold ham. The basis can be kept bottled in the refrigerator for flavouring mayonnaise.

---- ❖ ❖ ❖ ----

Here all the summer could I stay,
For there's Bishop's teign
And King's teign
And Coomb at the clear Teign's head—
  Where close by the stream
  You may have your cream
All spread upon barley bread.

Then who would go
Into dark Soho
And chatter with dank-haired critics,
  When he can stay
  For the new-mown hay,
And startle the dappled crickets?

JOHN KEATS

Evelyn Holding

Chairman, Standing Conference of Women's Organisations, Exeter, 1970.
Chairman, Senior Citizens' Organisation (St. Thomas, Exeter).

Croissants, *for our twin-town visitors, Rennes, France.*

Make a moderately soft, well-mixed dough, using the following ingredients:

14 oz plain flour	¾ oz yeast
Pinch salt	8 oz approx. milk (slightly warm)
1 egg yolk	1 oz butter
1 beaten egg for brushing	

Method. Place the flour and salt into a large basin or bowl. Rub in the butter. Place the yeast in a separate basin and add the egg yolk and warm milk. Mix these items thoroughly and add to the flour, butter and salt mixture. Mix to a smooth dough. Cover the dough with a clean cloth and allow to stand in a warm place for 30 minutes. Mix the dough in the bowl after 15 minutes' standing time, and cover again.

Roll out the dough approximately ⅛ in. thick and from the sheet of dough cut triangles about 5 in. from the base to the apex. Brush off surplus flour, then brush each triangle with softened butter. Roll up the triangles from the base to apex and bend to crescent shapes. Place on greased baking tins and brush lightly with egg. Allow to stand 20–25 minutes in a warm place. Bake in 450°F, Gas 8, until golden brown.

Makes approximately 16 croissants.

Gougere (using Choux pastry).

Gougère:

2 oz butter	4 oz flour (just under)
3 eggs (beaten)	⅜ pint water
2 oz diced cheese, seasoning	

Method. Melt butter, add water and bring to boil, add sifted flour all at once. Cook until mixture leaves the sides of the pan, and cool slightly. Gradually add the beaten eggs, and beat. Add diced cheese and seasoning. Well butter an ovenproof dish, 10 in. by 10 in. Arrange the choux paste around the dish. For a smaller dish, halve the quantities for the paste. Place filling in the centre. Mix grated cheese and breadcrumbs and sprinkle on top.

Filling:

½–1 lb cooked meat, poultry, fish, fresh or smoked	½ oz butter
1 dessertspoonful flour	1 medium onion
2 tomatoes	1 gill milk
1 tablespoonful finely grated cheese	1 teaspoonful chopped parsley
	1 tablespoonful browned crumbs

Method. Soften chopped onion in butter, add flour and milk to make sauce. Bring to boil, cook 2 minutes, add meat or fish, parsley and shredded tomato. Bake 400°F–425°F, gas 6–7 for 30–40 minutes. It should be well-risen and golden brown. Sprinkle with chopped parsley before serving.

Henrietta Holmes

Henrietta, Dartington College of Arts, Totnes.

Henrietta's job at Dartington, embraces the running of the White Hart dining-room, where all the staff is catered for, the visiting celebrities, and the many adult education courses; and also of the student dining-room where some 220 residential students are fed to a standard better than most three star hotels.

Henrietta (or Mrs Holmes) the Catering Officer, is an artist in food and a professional painter. She holds many medals including an International gold medal won at Hotelympia. She exhibits in many places in the country and on the continent.

'I could supply many recipes but think this one may prove helpful to many people who wonder why their beautiful freshly caught salmon doesn't taste so wonderful as it looked!'

Our way of Cooking Salmon at Dartington

Method. Slit the salmon carefully along its underside. Take out all the 'innards' and wash well. Dry off with tissues. Then, carefully nick through the backbone at the neck and tail. Ease with your fingers each rib bone separately and you will be surprised how cleanly it can be freed. Now, in the same manner, ease out the backbone, helping with a knife, if necessary. All the bones except the fins will come away in one skeleton.

Now rub the inside of the fish with salt, sprinkle with pepper, and then with finely chopped onion and mushroom which have been cooked in butter till just done. At this stage we also sprinkle with very little dry spring vegetable soup. Then we add dots of butter all over, about 3 oz, and lastly, sprinkle with wine, preferably dry white wine.

Close up the fish neatly so that it looks completely whole and untouched. Place on a piece of transparent oven foil, large enough to make a parcel of the fish. Pour over another cupful of wine and fold the parcel being careful to keep the fish in position—turn up the ends of the parcel to keep in the wine and secure them.

Place in steamer and cook for 45 minutes for a large salmon. Turn off the heat and leave another 15 minutes. Cool off, still wrapped in its parcel so that the juices can be absorbed.

Fish done in this way will always be moist and full of flavour and can be garnished as desired.

We usually serve 'en belle vue'. We carefully skin the upper side to expose the lovely salmon colour, and coat with aspic. We set it on a bed of clear aspic and garnish with sliced cucumber, hard boiled egg and King prawns, glazed with aspic, and set round it all manner of 'bits and pieces', like cooked cucumber baskets, tomato 'lilies' filled with peas, mushrooms filled with macédoine, etc.

Any left over aspic, coloured red or green and made stiff, can be chopped up roughly and piled in little heaps to catch the light.

By the way, a stiff lemon jelly flavoured with a little vinegar is a far better glaze for flavour than aspic proper.

Have you tried mixing horseradish with salad cream to dress the fish? It is incredibly good.

Helen M. Hore

Budleigh Salterton.

These recipes have been handed down to me from my great grandmother, Mary Chaster, mother of a former Mayor of Totnes and resident of Westhill House. They have been used in Devon for at least 150 years.

Christmas Pudding

1 lb Beef suet	1 lb raisins
1 lb currants	1 lb sultanas
1 lb Demerara or Barbados sugar	½ lb plain flour
¾ lb white breadcrumbs	2 oz mixed peel
½ nutmeg (grated)	1 oz allspice or mixed spice
2 lemons (grated rind and juice)	5 eggs
1 teacupful brandy or rum	1 tablespoonful black treacle

Method. Grate suet with a little flour. Wash fruit, dry well and chop raisins and sultanas small. Chop peel very finely, add sugar and put all into a large basin. Mix flour and grated breadcrumbs, nutmeg, spice and grated lemon rind, add these to basin and stir very well. Beat eggs and large cup milk, treacle, lemon juice, brandy or rum. Add to dry mixture and if too dry, add more milk. Stir very well and leave overnight. Stir again and, if necessary, add some more milk. Put into three medium basins or four small, cover with greasy papers and cloths and steam for 6 hours. (The cloth can be wrung out in boiling water and sprinkled with flour; floury side placed on greasy papers, helps to prevent water entering.) They can be cooked in ordinary saucepans but be sure no water gets in—just keep filling up with boiling water to about three-quarters up the sides of the basins. Remove cloths when cooked, re-cover with clean ones, and keep in a cool dry place. Boil or steam for four hours on Christmas Day or when wanted.

Five Cup Pudding

1 teacup each:- S.R. flour	Brown sugar
Raisins cut up or currants	Finely grated suet
Milk	

Method. Mix well, turn into well-buttered basin, leaving about 1 in. from top. Steam 2 hours or more and serve with hot custard.

Gingerbread

1 lb plain flour	2 dessertspoonsful ground ginger
½ lb Demerara or Barbados sugar	2 teaspoonsful bi-carbonate of soda
½ lb Fowler's black treacle	dissolved in 1 teacupful milk
½ lb butter (not margarine)	1 egg well beaten
2 dessertspoonsful allspice	

Method. Put flour in mixing bowl with ginger and spice. Put sugar, syrup and butter in saucepan over low heat till melted, but do not boil. Add hot liquid to flour. Mix well, then add egg and milk, beat well in. It should be very moist like thick batter, if not, add more milk and stir in well. Put in flat greased tin, about 12 in by 10 in by 2 in, in centre of hot oven gas 6, 400°F till well risen, then lower heat to gas 2, 300°F, for ½ hour. Leave in tin to cool.

Professor W. G. Hoskins

Exeter.

'One still eats best at home, and it is a minor torture to be compelled to eat out. English food at its best is the equal of anything anywhere in the world, and infinitely better than most countries. But it takes a good housewife to make it so, and such a wife is nowadays a pearl among women: indeed rarer than a pearl.'

Professor Hoskins, *Shell Guide to Leicestershire,* 1970.

Pigeon à La Flamande—for two persons.

2 pigeons	1 oz butter
2 rashers fat bacon cut in strips	6 small onions
½ pint stock	Salt and pepper
2 oz raisins (stoned, if necessary)	Beurre manié

Method. Heat butter in casserole, brown pigeons on both sides, lift out on to a hot plate. Brown onions and bacon in the same butter. Split pigeons and put back into onions and bacon. Add enough stock to come three-quarters of the way up the birds. Season. Cook in a moderate oven for an hour, or until the birds are tender. While the birds are cooking, soak the raisins in warm stock for about half an hour, and add to the casserole. The gravy may be thickened with a little beurre manié. (Beurre manié is, butter and flour worked together on a plate, and added in small pieces by degrees to the dish. Proportion of butter slightly greater than that of flour.)

Marmalade Syllabub—for six people.

½ pint double cream	2 good tablespoonsful marmalade
Juice of 1 lemon	1 oz caster sugar
1 tablespoonful brandy	

Method. Mix marmalade, lemon, sugar and brandy with half of the cream, then add rest by degrees, and whip until thick. Garnish with chopped toasted almonds.

———❖ ❖ ❖———

Professor W. G. Hoskins has been described by a reviewer as 'that prince of local Historians'. He retired from the Chair of English Local History at the University of Leicester, the only one of its kind, in 1968; since then, in his native Devon, he has devoted himself to writing, and growing herbs for his wife's cooking. He is a lover of good food and wine and believes that the pigeon is an under-rated bird in this country, not appreciated half as much as it is abroad. 'Fortunately, in a way, as this means that they are still relatively cheap to buy, but it usually needs dressing up in casserole form, and of the many possible ways of doing this, Pigeon à La Flamande is one of the best. A Marmalade Syllabub makes an excellent pudding to follow—a light dish after the heavy rich fare of the pigeon'.

Arthur Hutchings, Esq.

Professor of Music, Exeter University.

Two Local Cheese Recipes from Parkham, Nr Hartland.

Both of these were favourites with us when boys during the First War. As neither we, nor our friends, who also liked them, were well off, and as food was both scarce and expensive (even in Devon farm country) during the First World War, they are not expensive. I cannot explain their titles, but they were still used in Hartland and Morwenstow among old friends I visited about eight years ago.

Donkey Pie (*Possibly so called because oats were used with the cheese. To-day we can use any kind of 'rolled oats'.*)

Method. Line a shallow tin with thin pastry. Grate 2 oz cheese and mix it thoroughly with 4 oz rolled oats. Mix in with this a dessertspoonful of water and a teaspoonful ready-made mustard, with salt and pepper to taste, and not quite ½ oz margarine, melted. Spread evenly over the pastry, and cover with a very thin pastry 'lid', nicking the edges as usual. Bake in a moderate oven for about ½ hour.

Dodgers (*We liked these better than the pancakes which, in those days, were absolutely 'de rigueur' on Shrove Tuesday. They are a kind of cheese 'Yorkshire pudding'.*)

Method. Mix together two heaped tablespoons of flour and 2 teaspoonsful of fine oatmeal, with 2 level teaspoonsful of baking powder and a pinch of salt, or perhaps two. Beat into this enough liquid to make a firm batter which runs very slowly off the spoon. Not much liquid is needed—you can use milk or water. Add to the batter, cheese chips—ratio ½ cup of cheese chips to a cup of batter. This can be prepared the night before if you wish. Pepper and a few mixed herbs should be added at the time just before cooking. Drop tablespoonsfuls of the mixture into a frying pan of hot fat. Flatten each portion slightly. Fry slowly on each side over a low flame.

(*These, like the Saffron Cake, are in my Aunt Polly's handwriting: I am glad my wife got hold of her slips of paper.*)

Saffron has become expensive since the war, and this recipe gives the minimum amount. It is quite adequate to give the distinctive and delicious flavour, but can be increased where saffron is still obtainable from old-established grocers. It seems unobtainable in supermarkets, and the farther one goes from the parts of Devon and Cornwall, west of Exeter, the more one is likely to be forced to get saffron from the chemist instead of the grocer, and at a higher price.

The true saffron yeast cake of the West Country should not be confused with travesties sold under the same name. They are not yeast cakes and they often have no saffron, but are coloured yellow and have a disgusting sickly taste of vanilla and far too much sweetening.

Saffron Cake, Professor Hutchings' Aunt Polly's, from her manuscript recipes from Hartland, North Devon.

1 oz yeast (dried yeast will *not* do)	2 lb plain flour
4 oz lard	4 oz butter or margarine
12 oz fruit	2 oz peel
8 oz sugar	$\frac{1}{4}$ teaspoonful mixed spice
$\frac{1}{4}$ dram saffron	Pinch salt
$\frac{1}{2}$ pint milk	

Method. (a) *The Leaven.* Break up the yeast and mix with 2 heaped table-spoonsful flour. Add $\frac{2}{3}$ teacupful warm water in which a teaspoonful of sugar has been stirred. Mix all again and place in a warm corner, free from draught. It should rise in $\frac{1}{2}$ hour.

(b) *The Saffron.* This should have stood overnight cut up very finely, in a teacup half-filled with warm water.

(c) *The Mixture.* Put the 2 lb of flour in the mixing bowl and add sugar, spice and the pinch of salt. Rub in the fats until no lumps are left. Now add the Leaven, which has stood for $\frac{1}{2}$ hour and risen. Warm the milk and pour the saffron liquid into it. (Do not remove the little bits of saffron.)

Pour this into the cake dough. Mix thoroughly and let the basin stand for 4 hours in a warm place, and covered with a blanket or other warm cloth.

The cooking is as for bread, and the saffron cake should look like a loaf. It must not be over-cooked, 425°F, Gas No. 7, about 40 minutes.

In Queen Elizabeth I's reign, Trading Captains were told 'to try what vent you may have of Saffron, because this realme yeelds the best of the world, and for the tillage and other labours may set the poore greatly in worke to their reliefe.'

Richard Hakluyt, 1553–1616.

Saffron, used in Spain in savoury dishes, is used in the West Country in cakes. It was used in medicine in many countries. Hippocrates in Athens, the Father of Medicine, born nearly 2,500 years ago, mentioned it, and Homer, born nearly 2,800 years ago referred to it. The Chinese and many other races used it for cooking and medicine. Its dye was a royal colour in Ancient Greece. In an English leech-book of the tenth century it is mentioned; its cultivation gave Saffron Walden in Essex, its name. Our expensive pinch of saffron in our kitchens gives us a direct link with ancient civilisations.

Mr & Mrs Michael James

London, N.W.11.

Mr James is the architect for the new block of Y.W.C.A. Residential Flats in Exeter, in aid of which this book was first planned.

Leek and Bacon Pie

1 lb leeks	3 slices of best bacon
2 eggs	¼ carton double cream
6 oz short-crust pastry	

Method. Wash leeks thoroughly. Cut in half lengthways and put in saucepan with a knob of butter and 2 tablespoonsful water, and allow to simmer for 7 minutes. Drain and transfer leeks into pie dish and sprinkle over them the chopped bacon and the eggs well beaten and seasoned with salt and pepper and then pour the double cream over the mixture and cover with pastry. Put into pre-heated oven Mark 6 for 40 minutes (370°F–400°F).

Mince and Rice

1 lb best minced beef	3 green peppers, seeded
1 lb juicy tomatoes	1 large onion
Knob of butter	Dessertspoonful olive oil

To be eaten with boiled rice, i.e. 8 oz Patna

Method. Rice, just covered with boiling water and salt added, boiled until almost cooked. Transfer to a colander, place over a pan of hot water and cover with a cloth closely. The rice can be kept over very low heat for several hours until needed and the grains will be separate.

Heat butter and olive oil in saucepan. Chop onion and add it to the oil allowing it to cook gently for 5 minutes. Cut peppers into quarters and put into saucepan together with the tomatoes and minced beef and season well. Half cover mixture with water or stock and once brought to the boil allow to simmer for approximately 2 hours.

This is an original recipe given to Mrs James' family by a Spanish forbear.

Miss Evelyn Joynt, M.B.E.

National General Secretary, Y.W.C.A.

Recipe submitted by Lyn Joynt, 223 Latymer Court, London, W.6, Irish, single, globe-trotter. Works for the Y.W.C.A. and likes to spend her spare time sleeping, eating, walking (preferably in the sun), farming (particularly pigs) and painting (messily in oils).

One of my favourite recipes.

As a busy person I have very little time for elaborate cookery, yet I enjoy food and I enjoy entertaining my friends. I usually rely on the sensible casserole as main dish on my menus, since it can be prepared in tranquillity, cooked when needed, eaten when my guests choose to arrive and—very important—reheated (thoroughly) nightly to sustain me in solitary meals.

However, I like to start with something a little exotic before my casserole and here is one of my favourite starters.

Lavish Consomme

Required: 1 tin Consommé, 1 tin Caviare (*You can use 'Lump-Fish Roe'*, which costs approximately 4s. 6d. [22½p] a tin), Thick Devonshire Cream *Method.* The consommé should have been left in your refrigerator so that it is jellied and chilled. Turn it out into the required number of soup bowls. Next put a dollop of thick cream on top of the jellied comsommé. Finally top up the mixture with a spoonful of the caviare. Serve at once.

The result is delicious and puts your guests into a receptive state for the sober casserole to follow.

Mrs Mary Kneel

Streatham Drive, Exeter.

Lemonade

1 oz citric acid
2 lb granulated sugar

2½ pints boiling water
2 lemons

Method. Grate, cut and squeeze the lemons; place in a big bowl the rind and lemons with the citric acid and granulated sugar and pour over this the boiling water, stir until the sugar dissolves, and when cool add the lemon juice. Leave overnight. Strain into carefully washed screw-top bottles. This keeps well in a cool place for several weeks, and is very refreshing.

Christmas Pudding—*This is a very light pudding, which keeps well. It has stood the test for several generations of the family.*

1 lb 4 oz fresh white breadcrumbs
14 oz brown sugar
4 oz currants
1 oz chopped blanched almonds
4 oz mixed chopped peel
¼ wineglass brandy
½ pint pale ale

10 oz shredded suet
8 oz sultanas
8 oz raisins
¼ nutmeg grated
6 oz black treacle
2 oz self-raising flour

Method. Clean the fruit and mix all ingredients well in a big bowl. Cover and leave for 24 hours. Mix well again. If a little dry add more ale. The mixture should be moist, but not too wet. Spoon into well-greased pudding basins. This makes 5 small or 2 large puddings. Cover and tie with a cloth and steam for 3 hours, 4 hours for the larger ones. About 1 hour for re-heating. (Cover first with greased paper; dip cloth in boiling water and sprinkle with flour inside to make a waterproof covering; tie tightly.)

Mrs Kneel also gives Mrs Brook's biscuit recipe.

Mrs E. T. Brook

Mrs Brook makes large batches of these for the Parish Party, at St. Stephen's Church, Exeter. It isn't a party, it is claimed, without Mrs Brook's Chocolate Biscuits.

Method. Cream 4 oz butter and 2 oz caster sugar, work in 1 teacup self-raising flour, a small teacup dessicated coconut, and 1 teaspoonful cocoa. Spread this mixture on to a well-greased Swiss Roll tin and cook for about 25 minutes at 375°F, gas 5, until light brown. Remove from oven, and whilst still warm, spread 6 oz melted covering (couverture) chocolate over the top, and mark into slices with a sharp knife. Remove from tins when cold.

Mrs Marcus Knight

The Deanery, Cathedral Close, Exeter.

'I enclose three simple recipes which I use myself.'

Cream of Carrot Soup—(*serves six*).

3 large leeks
1 lb new young carrots
2 oz butter
¼ pint single cream

2 pints stock (or water with 2
  chicken cubes)
Salt and pepper
1 tablespoonful chopped parsley

Method. Trim green tops and base from leeks leaving about 1 inch of green top on each. Cut lengthwise, wash well and shred finely. Slice carrots thinly.

Melt butter and sauté vegetables gently. Stir in hot stock and simmer gently about 1–1½ hours. Liquidize or sieve; return to pan and bring almost to boiling point. Stir in cream and parsley.

Beef Goulash —(*serves four*).

1–1½ lb best stewing steak
1 oz dripping
1 (15 oz) tin tomatoes
1 bay leaf
1 level tablespoonful paprika
2–3 tablespoonsful soured cream
  (to be added last—optional)

Seasoned flour
1 onion peeled and sliced
1 small clove garlic
Salt and pepper
½ pint stock (or water and chicken
  cube)

Method. Trim fat and gristle off meat. Cut into neat pieces and roll in seasoned flour. Heat dripping in large pan, fry onion gently till soft and golden brown. Add meat and fry a little more quickly to brown. Stir in tomatoes, chopped garlic, bay leaf, salt and pepper, stock and paprika (or goulash seasoning). Lower heat, cover and simmer gently for 2½–3 hours or put in gentle oven.

Lemon Souffle

Method. Cream 1 cup of sugar with a tablespoon of butter. Add 2 tablespoons flour, the juice and grated rind of 1 lemon, a cup of milk, and the beaten yolks of 2 eggs.

Just before pouring into baking dish fold in the egg whites stiffly beaten. Set the dish in one filled with hot water and bake slowly till custard is set —about 1 hour.

It should have a light fluffy soufflé on top, and a creamy custard underneath.

Miss K. Elizabeth Kynaston

Exeter.

Miss Kynaston was Hon. Sec. of University College Club of Exeter 1926–1939, and President of the Exeter University Club 1962. She has been Hon. Sec. of the Exeter Branch of the National Council of Women since 1960, and is a Founder Member of the branch.

Favourite Chocolate Sponge—*(originally from Canada)*.

4 oz flour	4 oz sugar
2 eggs	1 teaspoonful baking powder
1 tablespoonful treacle	1 teaspoonful coffee
4 oz margarine	6 tablespoonsful milk or water
2 tablespoonsful cocoa	

Method. Cream margarine, sugar and treacle. Add eggs, mix well, and gradually add flour, cocoa, baking powder, and coffee, alternately with milk or water. Bake in two sponge tins, gas 5, 375°F, middle of oven, for 20 minutes. When cold fill cake with the following:

Filling:

2 oz margarine	1 tablespoonful treacle
2 tablespoonsful cocoa	½ teaspoonful vanilla

Method. Cream together over very low heat, and spread when cool.

❖ ❖ ❖

Devonshire Splits

1 lb McDougalls' extra-fine plain flour	1 teaspoonful caster sugar
½ teaspoonful salt	1 oz butter or margarine
½ oz yeast	½ pint skimmed milk, or ¼ pint milk and ¼ pint water

Method. Sieve the flour and salt into a basin. Cream the yeast with a little tepid milk and dissolve the butter gently in the rest of the milk. Pour all into the centre of the flour and mix to a dough. Put to rise in a warm place for 1 hour. Cut in twelve pieces, knead each to a ball, then flatten into a round ½ in. thick with the hands. Allow to prove for 20 minutes on a warm greased and floured baking tin. Brush with milk and bake in a hot oven for 15–20 minutes. Cut through, spread with butter or Devonshire Cream and serve hot. If preferred cold, sandwich them with jam and Devonshire Cream. 425°F, Gas mark 7.

The Viscountess Lambert

Spreyton, Crediton, Devon.

Devon Junket and Cream

Method. Make a junket in a round glass dish, then in a dish which is exactly the same size, make some Devonshire cream. When the cream is well-set very carefully lift the crust and place it on top of the junket. You can, if you wish, flavour the junket with a little rum or sherry and grated nutmeg, before putting the cream crust on.

A Victorian manuscript book of recipes gives one or two instructions in this inherited Devonshire recipe.

Junket. 1½ pints new milk made warm. Stir in a tablespoonful fine white sugar, pour it into a glass dish. Stir gently in, a tablespoonful of rennet, rather more than less. Stand in a warm place until set, which should be about ten minutes. When cold put nutmeg, rum according to taste, and a layer of cream on the top. It should be made an hour before . . . but should be ready for use then.

The manuscript notes on Lympstone by the late Miss M. E. Howard, born *c.* twenty years after the accession of Queen Victoria, are quoted by Mrs M. E. Scott in *Transactions, Devonshire Association*, vol.lxxxviii (1956), p. 254. I am indebted to Miss Theo Brown for finding this note for me. 'Another very pleasant amusement of those far-off days of the opening years of the reign of Queen Victoria, was the custom of "junketing", as it was then called. Young men and maidens would visit nearby farms where they ate junket in the true Devon way, with plenty of rum or brandy and nutmeg, and of course with cream. Gulliford Farm on the Exmouth road was a favourite place for this pleasant pastime.'

Miss C. L. Mayo, *granddaughter of Mrs Stoyle of Noss Mayo, remembers hearing that her grandmother went with friends to the Three Towns Dairies, Westwell Street, Plymouth, in 1830–40, to eat junket, as we meet for coffee to-day.*

Miss S. Large

The Rectory, Clyst St. George, Exeter.

Orange Surprise Summer Pudding

4 oranges   2½ oz whipped cream

Method. Cut the top of the oranges and scoop out the fruit. Cut fruit into pieces and mix with sliced strawberries. Replace into orange cases put some cream on each, and lids on top. Put on dish garnished with leaves.

Joan Innes Lennard

Chittlehamholt Manor, Umberleigh.

Mrs Lennard was, before her marriage, on the stage. She appeared in London, and America, and toured in the East. She has lived in Devonshire for the past twenty-three years, and is a magistrate, a member of the W.R.V.S., Chairman of the Exeter and North Devon Family Planning Association Clinics, and also of the Devon Branch of the South West Guernsey Cattle Breeders' Association.

Bass with Mushrooms and Prawns

Bass is an unusual fish found often in South Devon.

2 lb Bass	4 oz mushrooms
¼ pint fish stock made from the bones	Seasoning
4 tomatoes skinned and sliced	Walnut of butter
Chopped parsley	

Method. Skin fillets of Bass and arrange with sliced mushrooms in well-buttered ovenproof dish. Pour over stock, season, cover with well-buttered paper and poach in moderate oven for about 15 minutes. Cook sliced tomatoes in ovenproof dish with butter, and covered with buttered paper, in oven for 7 minutes or less, if ready sooner. Keep fish and tomatoes warm while making sauce.

Sauce

1 onion or shallot	1 oz butter
1 tablespoonful flour	½ pint milk
2 tablespoonsful cream	4 oz shelled prawns

Method. Cook onion (or shallot) in fish liquor from cooked Bass, and reduce. Strain and keep liquor. Melt butter in same pan, stir in flour and milk as for white sauce. Season, add fish liquor and onion. Boil well. Add prawns and cream. Put fish and mushrooms on to tomatoes and cover with sauce. Sprinkle with chopped parsley.

Devonshire Apple in and out

6 oz flour	4 oz sugar
4 oz fat	1 egg
1 lb apples	

This can be baked or steamed.

Method. Rub fat into flour, add sugar and beat in egg. Peel and slice apples into the mixture.

To bake—place in greased dish. Cook at 350°F, gas 4, for 25–30 minutes; it is equally good hot or cold.

To steam—put in greased basin, cover with greased paper, twisted on to rim, and steam for 1¼ hours. Eat hot. Serve both with brown sugar and Devonshire cream.

Devonshire Cider Fruit Cup

1 large bottle Devon cider
2 small bottles ginger ale
2 small bottles tonic water
1 tin grapefruit juice
½ pint (or a tin) orange juice,
   fresh if available

1 small bottle maraschino cherries
decorate with strips of cucumber
   skin and slices of orange and
   lemon

Method. Mix ingredients together in a large bowl with strained cherries. Pour into glass jugs and garnish. Makes 16 glasses.

Anne Thompson

Chittlehamholt Manor, Umberleigh.

Miss Anne Thompson is the actress daughter of Mr and Mrs Lennard of Chittleham-holt, and was educated at Greenways, Tiverton, and Drama School, Bristol. Has since appeared in Television, Radio and stage productions, including those directed by Peter Hall, John King and Robert Knight. Has also done modelling in London and Devon.

Trout Wayside Inn

Clean and trim the fish, lay in a shallow dish, and season lightly. Cover with cider, bring to the boil and simmer gently for 10 minutes. Place the fish on a dish and make the sauce from cider in which the fish was cooked, thickening it with a little butter and flour. Add some finely chopped gherkins to the sauce, and pour over the fish.

Duck Roasted in Honey

1 large duck (5–6 lb)
Juice of ½ a lemon
Stock made from giblets (excluding
   liver)

2 tablespoonsful honey
1 tablespoon arrowroot mixed
   with 2 tablespoonsful water, or
   stock

Stuffing (normal sage and onion stuffing, to which nuts can be added, grated rind of a lemon, juice of half a lemon, pinch of cinnamon, and a beaten egg). *Method.* Stuff the duck and rub over with a little butter. Spread the honey over the duck and roast 15 minutes to the lb, and 15 minutes extra. Baste occasionally. 400°F, gas 6. Remove duck, pour off fat. Mix sediment with lemon juice and stock. Bring to the boil, season, and thicken with arrowroot, i.e. mix the arrowroot with a little cold stock and pour the boiling liquid in, then return to pan for a few minutes.

J. Lethbridge

Exeter.

This family business of Poulterer and Game dealer was established in 1886. Mr Lethbridge remembers that cider was used for cooking in Devonshire more often than it is to-day.

Roast Venison

Method. Marinate joint 2–3 days, in either Cider, Vinegar and a little water, Vinegar and Wine, or Cider Vinegar.

To cook. Grease hands and grease joint with hands. Take 1 wineglass vinegar to 5 glasses of cider or wine. Slice 1 or 2 large carrots, 2 onions, chopped parsley, bay leaf and thyme. Cook together in the chosen liquid. Strain, and pour over joint. Cook joint in very hot oven, e.g. 1 hour for 5–6 lb.

Make gravy from sauce, adding red or white wine. Double cream may also be added if desired.

Casserole of Venison—For 4 persons.

2 lb prime venison from haunch or hind leg, cut into tidy pieces, with skin and gristle removed.

Method. Twenty-four hours before cooking prepare the marinade from cider, 1 or 2 onions, spice, juniper berries, cloves, peppercorns, salt. Place meat in large bowl, layered with sliced onions, spices, salt, and cover with cider. Leave 24 hours in a cool place.

Remove from marinade, dry the meat and shake it in flour in a paper bag, to coat the pieces. Keep the marinade liquor after straining it. Fry the meat in butter and oil to seal it, and until the flour is brown. Place in casserole. Add 8 oz mixed diced vegetables, e.g. carrots, celery, young white turnips, three tablespoonsful chopped onion, bay leaf, sprig thyme, 6 peppercorns, a pinch of salt, 1 or 2 grains Cayenne pepper.

To the sediment in the pan, add a little more flour if necessary, make into smooth roux, gradually add 2½ cups marinade liquor, or more, stir until smooth. Pour over meat and vegetables. Simmer in low oven for about 3 hours. Gas 3, 325°F. Remove from oven and add 1 glass of any wine or port.

Serve with creamed potatoes, redcurrant jelly and any green fresh vegetable; curly kale or brussels sprouts are specially good. This can be cooked the day before, and brought to piping hot temperature when wanted.

Mrs Basil Lindsay-Fynn

Lee Ford, Budleigh Salterton.

Lee Ford is an essentially friendly house and seems to greet every visitor with its own warm welcome. It is simple in pattern with a restrained elegance which grows with age. Thus simple food of good quality matches its charm and the following method of cooking potatoes has been much enjoyed by our family and guests for generations.

Potatoes a la Maison

Method.   Potatoes boiled and strained and put through a mouli then returned to the saucepan in which a suitable knob of butter has been melted. Add milk, grated cheese, a generous amount of Devonshire cream, salt and black pepper. Mix well. Fry diced bacon until really crisp and cover the potatoes in their serving dish with this and some chopped parsley. Quantities depend on how many are to be served, how much cheese is liked and the Devonshire cream can be replaced by the cream of other counties, though it is never as good.

Japonica Jelly

To serve with cold meat for a summer lunch or supper.

Method.   Wipe fruit and cut into quarters. Put into saucepan with sufficient water barely to float fruit, cook gently, covered, until soft. Strain through fine cloth or jelly bag overnight. Allow 1 lb granulated sugar to pint juice. Bring juice to boil with lid on, add sugar and boil, stirring with wooden spoon for about 15 minutes. Test with small spoonful on cold plate: if it wrinkles it is set. Put in small jars.

Mrs F. J. Llewellyn

Wife of Vice-Chancellor, Exeter University.
Member of Y.W.C.A. Development Committee, Exeter.

Cod Roe Paste

For sandwiches, canapés and hors d'oeuvre.
2 medium-sized roes (large ones tend to be coarse, and small ones too time-consuming to prepare).

Method. Simmer gently for about 20 minutes in a covered saucepan with bay leaf, mace and peppercorns. Lift on to a warm dish. While still hot remove skin with knife and fork. Put roe into warm basin and break up with fork. Add plenty of butter, anchovy essence, tarragon vinegar, lemon juice, powdered mace, ground black pepper. Do not make too liquid.

Beat together with a fork, or an electric blender, for 2 minutes. Press into small jars. Keep in a cool place and use within a couple of days.

Cod Roe Spread—*for family lunch or supper.*

Method. Make as above, but cut down on butter and added flavours. Press into an old-fashioned soup plate, previously buttered, cover with a dinner plate and leave in a cool place overnight. When required, turn plates upside down, shake, remove soup plate. Top of roe may be simply decorated with thin slices of stuffed olive and strips of fillet of anchovy. Serve with thinly sliced buttered wholemeal bread, celery hearts and watercress.

Blackberry and Elderberry Jam

Method. Gather fully ripe elderberries. Weigh empty saucepan. Remove berries from stalks with a fork, allowing them to fall into saucepan. Add blackberries in roughly equal volume to elderberries. Weigh again. Add 1 tablespoonful of water, put lid on saucepan, bring slowly to the boil, and keep just on the boil for 15–20 minutes.

Have ready in oven, warmed sugar in proportion of 12 oz to 1 lb fruit. Add warmed sugar to near-boiling fruit. Stir all together gently with wooden spoon and bring to boil again, keeping at a steady boil for 20 minutes, or more vigorously for 15 minutes.

Cider Rum Punch—*for a party at Christmas time.*

1 large sweet orange 　　　　　　　　1 tangerine 　1 lemon

Method. Peel these with a potato peeler, so that no white pith is removed; or peel, lay peel flat on a board, shiny side down, and with a sharp knife scrape away the pith. Chop peel finely, and put in small saucepan. Add fruit sliced, with pith and pips removed. Finally, add 1 good teaspoonful of ground cinnamon, or equivalent in essence, 12 cloves, 4 heaped tablespoons light brown sugar, 1 teacup water, 1 wineglass ginger-wine. Simmer, covered, very gently for 30 minutes. Into a large saucepan, pour 3 quarts sweet cider. Strain the liquid contents of small saucepan, pressing with back of wooden spoon. Heat gently to drinking temperature, add $\frac{1}{2}$ bottle rum, re-heat gently. Avoid over-heating.

Lundy South Lighthouse

This is a recipe from the Lighthouse Keeper in Charge.

Lighthouse Flashers—*Children like these with Sunday dinner.*

Method. Peel and boil potatoes. When cooked mash and add butter and milk, salt and pepper. Form mashed potatoes into 3 in. towers, and bake in oven until brown, about 5–10 minutes. Top each tower with a glacé cherry and serve instead of conventional roast potatoes.

In 1819 the Corporation of Trinity House began to build a lighthouse on Lundy Island at the entrance to the Bristol Channel, and it was lighted for the first time in 1820. It was the first lighthouse in England to have a quick flashing light. Complaints that fog shrouded it completely at times, resulted in the building, in 1897, of two lighthouses, on the North and South extremities of the island. The Lighthouses are each manned by a Principal Keeper and three assistant Keepers, three of whom are always on duty at any one time, the fourth being on leave ashore.

The most famous lighthouse in the world is probably the Eddystone, built on a small and very dangerous rock, about 13 miles south of Plymouth. It was the first to be built on a small rock in the open sea, and the first one was completed in 1698. Eddystone is one of the most isolated in the world. The tower is 168 feet high, and the total weight of stone in the structure is 4,668 tons. The light can be seen for $17\frac{1}{2}$ miles.

These notes were furnished by Trinity House, London. Trinity House was granted its first Charter as a Corporation in 1514 by Henry VIII, and since then has evolved as a unique institution, with the prime motive the safety and well-being of the Mariner. Its main functions are (1) the General Lighthouse Authority for England and Wales, Channel Islands and Gibraltar, (2) the Principal Pilotage Authority in the United Kingdom and (3) a Charitable Organisation for the relief of certain seafarers and their dependants who have fallen upon hard times. The Lighthouse Service is responsible for fixed and floating seamarks and visual, audible and radio aids to navigation.

Trinity House maintains 88 Lighthouses, 33 Light Vessel Stations, and more than 600 buoys of which well over half are lighted.

Lundy South Lighthouse Keepers remind us that books forwarded to the G.P.O. nearest to the Lighthouses, are welcome, 'to offset the lonely hours'.

Mrs M. L. D. Macadam (*née* Amy Elton)

Royal Academy Schools Medallist, 1926.

Woodbury, Exeter.

I was in India for ten years and this recipe was used by a Goan cook. It is very useful for a party. I have an 'End of Session' party for my painting pupils and always feed them on this, and am usually asked for the recipe. For four people.

Egg Pillau—(or chicken pieces, or bacon. Belly of pork can be used in which case pork fat would be the frying agent). I cook on an Aga.

2 level tablespoonsful curry powder	6 oz rice
2 large onions	2 cloves garlic
4–6 oz butter	4 oz sultanas
4 oz raisins	5 eggs
1 lemon	Cinnamon, salt and pepper to taste

Method. (1) Boil the rice—hard boil the eggs.

(2) Using the hot plate, melt the butter in a large pan, peel and cut up onions and fry until transparent and slightly golden.

(3) Move to cool plate, add curry powder, lemon juice, garlic, sultanas and raisins and simmer for about 20 minutes. Chop eggs, add to the other ingredients, season and add rice. Return to hot plate, turning the whole about with spoon or fish slice for about 10 minutes. Serve with poppadums, mango chutney and desiccated coconut.

Anne McGahey

Penleonard Close, Exeter.

Smothered Mackerel

4 fresh mackerel	Parsley
2 tomatoes	1 medium onion, or 4 spring
1 lemon	onions (thinly sliced)
Bay leaf	Salt and pepper

Method. Thinly slice onion and tomatoes, and quarter the lemon. Cut four pieces of cooking foil large enough to wrap the fish loosely in. Place one mackerel on each, on a layer of onion and sliced tomatoes, and a small piece of bay leaf. Place a wedge of lemon on top, season well, sprinkle with parsley, and wrap each fish. Cook, moderate oven, 350°F, gas 4, 15–20 minutes.

Steak, Lemon Dressing

Fillet or rump steak, beaten flat to $\frac{1}{4}$ in. thick, and seasoned, with salt and milled pepper.

	2 tablespoonsful lemon juice
2 oz butter	Chopped parsley
1 tablespoonful very fine chopped onion	

Method. Fry steak in butter for 1–2 minutes each side. Remove and keep warm. Add lemon juice and chopped onion to residue in the pan. Cook quickly for 1 minute, stirring constantly, spoon on to steak, and sprinkle chopped parsley. Serve.

Miss E. Marsden

Y.W.C.A. Area Accountant.

Chocolate-Date Slice

4 oz margarine   2 oz caster sugar
1 packet (8 oz) stoned dates

Method. Put into largish saucepan and on a low heat until dates are mushy. Remove from heat. Add 4 teacupsful Rice Krispies and mix well. Press *well* into greased tin (Swiss Roll size). Top with about 7 oz melted cooking chocolate and allow to set.

Major H. Marsh

Property Development Officer of the Y.W.C.A., Great Britain.

2, Weymouth Street, London, WIN 4AX.

Contributed by Major Marsh, Late the Middlesex Regiment (Duke of Cambridge's Own, commonly known before 1881 as H.M. 57th Foot, or 'The Die Hards').

The Contented Chap's Casserole

Method. One 3–4 lb chicken, or 1½ lb steak or shin beef, or oxtail. If beef or oxtail, cut into neat pieces. Place chosen meat into casserole and cover with half bottle wine, and 1 tablespoonful Worcester Sauce.

Add contents of 1 tin new potatoes and carrots, 1 chopped onion, 8 oz chopped mushrooms. Add seasoning.

Cover the casserole, place in oven for about 2 hours, 300–350°F, gas 3.

I can assure you that nothing except the bones will be thrown away at the end of this meal and this should be sufficient for three or four normal people.

Having been the reluctant guest for nearly four years of the Emperor of Japan from 1941–1945, and because during that period our basic diet was half a pound of rice per day, it was necessary to organise a vegetable garden in the early days of our captivity, so that before the end of the war the vegetable farm covered an area of over 2 acres, and provided the 500 or more British and Allied prisoners of war in Argyle Street Camp, Kowloon, Hong Kong, with over one and a half tons of fresh vegetables. The above dish is nutritious and needs only about 10 minutes to prepare.

The Hon Robin Maxwell-Hyslop, M.P.

Mr Maxwell-Hyslop was born at Ivybridge, Devon, in 1931, and he and his wife live next door to the blacksmith's forge at Silverton. Before election as Member for Tiverton in 1960 he worked at Rolls-Royce Aero-Engine Division in Derby. Captain in the Royal Artillery (Territorial Army).

Parson's Nose

Method. Place in a bottle the peel of half a lemon, taking care to avoid the pith. Add two shakes of Angostura bitters and a tablespoonful each of peach bitters and orange bitters.

Fill up the bottle with equal quantities of brandy and ginger wine. After a week, strain into another bottle. Your 'Parson's Nose' is now ready for drinking and you can throw away the advertisements for central heating systems!!

(*Mr Maxwell-Hyslop considers that 'Whiteways ginger wine as well as being made in Devon, has quite the best flavour and texture'.*)

———❖—❖—❖———

Devonshirish Coffee

Assemble in the following order in a warmed container:

Sugar (Preserving crystals for preference) dissolved in 1 finger Irish whisky, add hot black coffee.

Pour gently on top, Devonshire double cream, or preferably Devonshire clotted cream; pouring it over, or allowing it gently to slide off, a spoon. Don't stir.

———❖—❖—❖———

Give me that man, that dares bestride
The active sea-horse, and with pride
Through that huge field of waters ride:
Who, with his looks too, can appease
The ruffling winds or raging seas
In midst of all their outrages.
This, this a virtuous man can doe,
Saile against Rocks, and split them too;
Ay, and a world of Pikes pass through.

Robert Herrick, *Vicar of Dean Prior, Devon, near Totnes.*
Born 1591, died 1674.

71

Miss C. L. Mayo

Miss Mayo is the granddaughter of the late Mrs Stoyle of Noss Mayo.

Breakfast Groats

This is a traditional Devonshire dish which is filling and delicious.

Method. Boil ½ lb groats (obtainable from Health Food Stores). Drain and season with salt, pepper and allspice. Mix in small pieces of Devon fat green bacon (about 1 in. square).

Fry all together in bacon fat in a frying pan, over low heat until bacon is cooked and its fat absorbed by the groats. If groats are not obtainable, pearl barley can be used, but is not nearly as good.

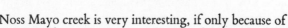

'Noss Mayo creek is very interesting, if only because of the keen rivalry and separatism between Noss on one side of the creek and Newton on the other, said to be due to the former being a Celtic settlement and the latter Anglo-Saxon. Every cottage seems to have its own landing stage, and the boats' painters pass in even through the bedroom windows, presumably being tied to the bedstead or the toe of some sleeping yachtsman. Except for one or two mouldering stone ruins and a pretty group of houses by the ferry, there is practically nothing to interrupt the soft sweep of the wooded hills which flank the whole of the tidal Yealm and its creeks upstream. One can see above the woods the far grey tors of Dartmoor.'

Under Sail Through Red Devon—Raymond B. Cattell, 1937.

The Hon. Mrs John Mildmay-White

Holbeton, Plymouth.

Poached Eggs in Cheese Souffle Sauce—*An enjoyable supper dish.*

7 eggs	6 rounds of dry bread
Butter and oil	2 tablespoons flour
Just over ½ pint milk	2 oz grated Gruyère cheese
Salt, pepper and cayenne	

Method. Poach 6 eggs and lay them to drain on soft paper. Fry the rounds of bread until golden brown in a mixture of butter and vegetable oil. Allow both to become cold. Half an hour before serving make the sauce. Melt 1 oz of butter and blend in the flour. Heat the milk and pour it in. Bring to the boil and simmer for about 3 minutes. Shake in the grated cheese off the fire and stir until melted. Season with pepper and salt and a little cayenne. Separate yolk and white of other egg, stir yolk into cooled sauce, and beat the white. Place the croutons in a fireproof dish and place a poached egg on each. Fold the whipped white into the sauce and spoon over the eggs. Place under a hot grill and cook for about 10 minutes.

Mr and Mrs C. R. Milne

The Harbour Bookshop, Fairfax Place, Dartmouth, South Devon.

Mr and Mrs C. R. Milne have been running the Harbour Bookshop in Dartmouth since 1951. After nineteen years they reckon to be very nearly Devonians, and would certainly never wish to live anywhere else. A busy business life does not leave a lot of time for leisure pursuits, but any hours that can be snatched are spent enjoying the unmatched pleasures of the Devon countryside and coast, or in taming their orchard garden. Holidays are usually spent in Italy, in a town very similar to Dartmouth, with steep steps, stone walls, old houses and very blue sea. Mrs Milne is a keen but erratic cook and Mr Milne an enthusiastic customer for good food. A love of Italy brings with it an appreciation of the Italians' preference for cooking with very fresh materials simply prepared, especially salads, fruit and vegetables. Here is Mrs Milne making a fuss about fish.

It seems a pity that visitors and residents too for that matter, in Devon, seldom get the chance to eat fresh locally caught fish in any other form than fried with chips. One can get cod and chips or plaice and chips anywhere. Surely in Devon one should be able to sample grilled mackerel fresh from the quay or a slice of baked bass? You stand a better chance of these in London. My fishmonger tells me that he sends his bass to London and a local crabbing firm exports its catch to the Continent. Unfair to Devon! We must make the best of it with home cooking.

One of our favourite fish is John Dory. This ugly looking creature is one of the best. An easy and delicious recipe is given below. If you can't get Dory, any firm white fish that will not break up in cooking will do. Bream is excellent. If the fishmonger fails you, frozen hake fillets are very good, if hardly Devonian.

Fish and Herbs

Method. Dry the fillets and dip in seasoned flour, using freshly ground black pepper. Heat a knob of butter with a little cooking oil in a heavy enamelled skillet or stoneware shallow dish. (Never cook with wine or cider in a plain metal pan.) Add some chopped herbs, preferably parsley, fennel leaves, marjoram or basil. Fry the fish gently on both sides for about 3 minutes, leaving the skin side uppermost. Squeeze on a little lemon juice. Add about half a wineglassful of dry cider, turn the heat to lowest possible and cover pan with a lid or foil. Simmer for about 10 minutes. Before serving, remove the skin from the fish and add a little thin cream or top of the milk. There should be only a small quantity of delicious savoury sauce. If this appears to be too liquid, add a little flour to thicken it. Serve straight from the pan.

Nicest accompaniments to this dish are new potatoes and a plain green salad. Or whole young French beans. Or peas from your garden. Drink some dry cider. Devon caterers are missing a good thing with cider, supposedly a local speciality. Try asking for some and you'll see what I mean—you'll be offered a sweet one, which is not much good, except for the children.

Alderman Mrs M. Nichols

Exeter.

I can assure you of my special interest in this project; it will help to meet the great need for this kind of accommodation in the City.

Alderman Nichols was the first woman to be appointed Sheriff and, later, Mayor of this City of Exeter.

Shortbread

7 oz flour	1 oz ground rice
4 oz butter or margarine	2 oz caster sugar
Pinch of salt	

Method. Soften butter, beat with sugar to a cream. Mix flour, ground rice and salt together and add to butter. Knead thoroughly until a soft dough is formed, free from cracks. Very slightly grease a mould (or sponge tin) and press the dough into it. Prick with a fork and score the edges.

Bake in a moderately hot oven for 45 minutes (gas Reg. 3, 330°F) when it should be biscuit colour. Turn out and cut into shapes while hot.

Remy Nicholson

Hon. Sec. Torquay Y.W.C.A. Quest Club.

Ginger Biscuits

4 oz butter or margarine	4 oz caster sugar
8 oz plain flour	½ teaspoonful bi-carb.
2 level teaspoonsful ground ginger	

Golden syrup—as much as will go on to about 3 in. of a table knife

Method. (1) Cream the butter, sugar and syrup.

(2) Sieve together the flour, ground ginger and bi-carb.

(3) Blend all the ingredients together—this will form into a firm 'paste'.

(4) Divide into halves and form each into a roll-like 'sausage'. Then, using a sharp knife, cut into slices, approximately ¼ in. or less thick and place on a baking tray. Oven heat—Gas 2, 300°F. Time for cooking about 15–20 minutes and slow cooking is essential.

Note: *Once these have been made and tasted you will need twice the quantity.*

Mrs R. North

who was born eighty-five years ago in Barnstaple, granddaughter of William Handcock, Barnstaple Coachbuilder.

Barnstaple Fair is held annually in September. Traditional foods are offered, and this is one of the fairings.

Gingerbread

6 oz treacle	8 oz flour
5 oz butter or margarine	6 oz sugar
Ground ginger (1 teaspoonful)	

Method. (1) Warm the treacle.
  (2) Rub fat into flour.
  (3) Add sugar and ginger.
  (4) Mix well, and blend with warm treacle.
  (5) Well grease tin, and place pieces the size of a small walnut an inch or two apart.
  (6) Bake 300°F, gas 2, for 10 minutes.

Lift on to wire tray, using palette knife or fish slice. Makes about 60.

Mr Sutherland of Barnstaple writes that 'Ginger fairings are still made and sold along with Toffee Apples and other scrumptious items'. He gives the following recipe for Brandy Snaps.

1 lb 4 oz flour	4 oz butter
½ oz ground ginger	4 oz white shortening
26 oz caster sugar	Pinch mixed spice
24 oz golden syrup	

Method. Sieve flour, ginger and spice. Rub in fats, add sugar and syrup. Mix thoroughly. Mould 2 oz pieces into rounds and place on well-greased baking sheets. Flatten each with the hand and bake at 350°F, gas 4, until golden brown. Drape around greased rolling pins whilst still warm. Store in airtight tin.

———— ❖ ❖ ❖ ————

'The eldest gingerbread was not a cake, but a solid slab of honey, baked with flour, ginger, etc. In the "Tournament" period it was a popular gift (rather like expensive chocolates to-day). Appropriately it seems to have been designed to copy cuir bouilli armour, being coloured a tawny brown with Saunders, polished (with egg white?), and decorated with clusters of six small box leaves, set to form a fleur-de-lis, and gilt-headed cloves, driven in like nails. The resemblance to a piece of tooled and gilt-studded leather was very effective.

This dark heraldic decoration was as appropriate to the early medieval period as the frilly white sugar icing is appropriate to the early Victorian period.'   DOROTHY HARTLEY, *Food in England.*

Saunders or Sanders is Red Sanders (*pterocarpus Santalina*), an inodorous dye-wood, not the fragrant sandal-wood.

There is a medieval Tilt Yard in the Gardens of Dartington Hall, Totnes.

Barbara Palmer

Brixham.

Old English Rhubarb Conserve

4 lb rhubarb cut into 1 inch pieces   5 lb sugar
1 lb stoned raisins   Grated rind and juice of 2 oranges
1 teaspoonful ground ginger   and 1 lemon

Method. Mix and allow to stand for ½ hour. Boil for 45 minutes, stirring constantly.

Put up into dry jars.

This comes from a book compiled from contributed recipes, published in 1830 and sold to raise funds for a new Methodist Sunday School building.

Mrs Palmer pioneered Writers' Circles in the South of Devon. She now has centres in Paignton, Totnes, Ashburton, Galmpton as well as her home town, Brixham, with close on a hundred students each year. (These classes are under the Adult Education winter programme of the Devon County Education Department).

※ ※ ※

'... Here I met the brown-sailed Brixham fishing fleet, standing in from sea, heavily-laden. The first three trawlers were as dead in line as cruisers at a Royal Review and were bearing straight down upon me. I debated whether I might construe the navigation rules to mean that they must give way to my cockleshell. True, they were close hauled on the starboard tack (to which port gives way) but I also was fairly close hauled on the same tack and might come under the heading of "ship overtaken" which must be avoided by those overtaking. I held straight on.

'A large and jovial face appeared over the bulwarks of the first boat—eyes somewhat bulbous with astonishment as they surveyed *Sandpiper.*

"Where be gwain tu in ee?"

"Dartmouth", I shouted.

This evidently struck him as a very ripe joke and his laughter brought a second surprised face to the side.

In a while I waved good-bye to my big brown friends.

"Mind the fishes doan't eat 'ee", was the Skipper's parting shot.

'I watched them sail into Brixham—dear old unchanging Brixham—"the haven under the hill"; home of the sturdiest and most spirited sons of Devon. Alike in the freshness of morning or when the chimney smoke gathers over the harbour valley in the coloured twilight, you will find the simple grey houses and the homely folk of Brixham a spectacle satisfying to the eye and to the heart.'

From *Under sail through Red Devon,*—RAYMOND B. CATTELL, 1937.

※ ※ ※

The Reverend Francis Lyte, Vicar of Brixham, worked with Brixham people, and knew their tough life, for twenty-five years. Not long before he died he prayed that he might be enabled to write a triumphant poem as a climax to his life's work, and on one of his last evenings in Brixham he went on to Berry Head at sunset and wrote the hymn, 'Abide with me'.

Mrs N. Parker

Greystones, Winkleigh, Devon.

Squab Pasty

6 oz self-raising flour
6–8 oz lamb (cooked or fresh)
1 apple

3 oz lard and margarine mixed
1 onion
Pepper and salt

Method. Make a stiff dough with flour and fat. Roll half and place in sandwich tin. Cut lamb into small pieces. Slice onion and apple finely and place on meat. Season. Roll out rest of pastry and place on top, pressing down the edges. Bake 10 minutes in hot oven, 375°F, gas 5, then put on bottom shelf for 35 minutes more.

Leek Pasty

6 oz self-raising flour
1 egg
2 leeks

3 oz lard and margarine mixed
3 rashers streaky bacon (green)
Little milk

Method. Cut leeks long ways, wash and leave to dry rolled in cloth. Rub fat into flour, add salt and a little water to make a stiff dough. Roll out half of it to fit sandwich tin, and line the tin. Remove rind from bacon and cut into thin slices, place on pastry. Cut leeks into thin slices, place on bacon, season. Beat egg with a little milk and pour over. Cover with the other half of the rolled out dough, pressing edges together. Bake 30 minutes at 350°F, gas 4, then put on bottom shelf for 15 minutes.

Spring onions and/or chopped parsley can be used instead of leeks.

Miss Dorothy Parnacott

Torrington.

Miss Parnacott's ancestor, Tristram Risdon, the famous antiquary, wrote 1605–1630, 'The Chorographical Description or Survey of the County of Devon'.

Cherry Loaf Cake

2 cupsful flour
½ teaspoonful salt
¾ cupful sugar
1 egg well beaten
¾ cupful milk

2½ teaspoonsful baking powder
4 oz butter
Little almond extract
½ cupful cherries, halved and
   pitted

Method. Mix all together and put in a greased cake tin. Bake in a slow oven for 1 hour.

Strawberry Shortcake

½ lb flour
4 oz caster sugar
2 teaspoonsful baking powder
1 lb strawberries

4 oz butter
½ teaspoonful salt
Little milk
Devonshire cream

Method. Sieve together flour, baking powder and salt, rub in the butter until the mixture resembles coarse meal. Add very gradually enough milk to give the mixture the consistency of a soft dough, working the liquid in with a knife. Toss the dough on to a floured board and divide into two round flat cakes, one for each sandwich tin. Bake in hot oven 15 minutes. Remove from oven. Prepare filling. Wash and hull strawberries and put aside sufficient number for decoration on top of cake. Mash the rest with a silver fork. Add caster sugar, leave until sugar is dissolved. Place half filling on one cake layer, place second layer on top and cover this with rest of filling. Decorate with whole strawberries. Pour juice round cake. Serve with Devonshire cream.

L. W. Lownds Pateman

Babbacombe and St. Marychurch.

Both these recipes have proved very popular when used as a Competition in our Charity Carnival Fair, which the Babbacombe and St. Marychurch Traders and Hoteliers Association has sponsored for the past sixteen years, and from which over thirty charities derive benefit.
Two local dishes.

St. Marychurch 'Scallops'

1 lb cooked potatoes
4 oz grated cheese
1 gill milk

¼ teaspoonful made mustard
1 teaspoonful chopped parsley
Sprinkling cayenne pepper
1 oz butter

Utensils. Sieve, wooden spoon, grater, scallop shells, basin, teaspoon and saucepan.

Method. Rub the potatoes through a sieve, melt the butter, add the sieved potatoes, parsley, grated cheese (leaving a little to sprinkle over the top), mustard and pepper, and beat thoroughly.

Put this mixture into sufficient buttered scallop shells, sprinkle with grated cheese and brown in a hot oven or under the grill.

Babbacombe Tart—For 4–6 persons.

8 oz grated apples
2 oz butter
6 sliced almonds
Grated rind of half a lemon

4 oz caster sugar
3 tablespoons milk
Short or puff pastry
Whipped whites of 2 eggs

Time to cook, about 20 minutes, gas 8, 450°F, for puff pastry; gas 5, 375°F, for short pastry.

Method. Line a pie tin with the pastry and cook. Mix the sugar and apples, melt the butter in the milk, stir it in, and add the rest of the ingredients. Sprinkle almonds on top. Turn into the pastry-lined tin and bake in a moderate oven.

Joe Pengelly

News Reader, B.B.C., Plymouth.

Mrs Pengelly's Slice

Method. Beat 4 oz butter and ¼ cup caster sugar to a cream. Add 1 beaten egg, then 1½ cups S.R. flour. Press mixture into a slab tin (about ½ inch depth—the mixture, not the tin). Spread with raspberry jam. Beat together 1 egg, half a cup sugar, 1 cup coconut, and spread on top of jam. Bake 15 minutes moderate oven and cut when cool.

Kay Pollock

Magdalen Road, Exeter.

Cheese Cake

Method. *Crust:* ½ lb plain digestive biscuits. 4 oz melted butter. Reduce the biscuits to crumbs and stir in melted butter. Line two sandwich tins with tin foil, paint with melted butter and press the crumb mixture over the bottom and sides.

Filling:

4 oz cream cheese	8 oz cottage cheese
1 teaspoonful vanilla	6 oz caster sugar
4 eggs	

Method. Mash together the cheeses, caster sugar and vanilla. When the ingredients are well blended, add the eggs, one at a time. Beat thoroughly until each egg is absorbed before adding the next. When mixture is smooth and airy, tip on to the crust.

Topping:

½ pint sour cream	1½ tablespoons caster sugar
¼ teaspoon vanilla	

Method. Stir ingredients until smooth and tip on cheese cake (cooled). Put in oven at 400°F (gas 6) for 5–6 minutes (until firm). Serve chilled.

Margaret Potts

'As I only came to live in Devon in 1956, I am still a "furriner",' writes Margaret Potts, who lives with her friend, Winifred Odell, in the Teign Valley, 'but I am devoted enough to wish to stay, and I found a home by chance, just inside the Dartmoor Park, and attached to the friendly village of Dunsford. We are both Quakers, and we attend Spiceland Meeting, which has a beautiful old Meeting House, dating from 1680, just outside Uffculme. It is on a site where George Fox preached earlier. We have enjoyed this cake recipe after meetings in Devon, and at Jordans, where Quakers met in the early seventeenth century, and we know it is used by Friends in Yorkshire and Warwickshire. It has no known name, so I will call it—Quaker Cake.'

Quaker Cake

1 rounded tablespoonful golden syrup	2 rounded tablespoonsful cocoa
3 oz butter or margarine	½ lb packet of Rich Tea, Marie or Osborne biscuits

Method. Melt syrup, butter and cocoa together and stir in crushed biscuits. Press into a rectangular dish or sandwich roll tin, to cool. When set pour over 6 oz melted chocolate or make icing or fudge to cover.

Mrs William Power

West Avenue, Exeter.

Mrs Power is an ardent worker for the Exeter Branch of Save the Children Fund. This recipe was given to me by Mrs Gillard of Bradninch. It is a traditional Devon recipe and her Mother-in-law used to say, 'You take a nice bit of flour, maid, and a nice bit of suet, and couple of "opples". When asked how much of each she would reply, "you know, maid, a nice little bit".' The following quantities are a more reliable guide.

Apple In 'n Out

8 oz self-raising flour   4 oz suet
About 3 good sized apples (Bramleys are best)
Pinch of salt   Milk to mix

Method. Cut the apples into small, thin pieces and mix with the flour and suet and salt. Add milk to a fairly soft consistency, put into a cloth, tie securely. Place in a saucepan of boiling water and boil for about 1 to 1½ hours. Serve with soft brown sugar and Devonshire clotted cream.

Mrs H. M. Pratt

Pennsylvania, Exeter.

This belonged to Mrs Pratt's Norwegian Mother, and is her own original recipe.

Pork Brawn

3lb pigs knees (or hand, or knuckle)   Hind leg 'knees' are best—or
    but NOT the trotters   ½ pigs head

Method. Wash, put in saucepan; pour over about 1 pint of cold, well-salted water and boil for about 3 hours, or until meat comes off the bones easily. Skim well. Pick meat off, remove the skin carefully and put a large piece at the bottom of a pie dish, skin side down. Cut the meat and fat in neat *small* strips and put in the dish with a good sprinkling of pepper, cloves and allspice, mixed together, between each layer.

Skim fat from the stock and add 1 to 1½ tablespoonsful wine vinegar. Now pour the stock while still hot, over the meat, and leave in a cold place until next day; turn out and stud surface with whole cloves before serving.

Lady Rayner

Ashcombe Tower, Near Dawlish, South Devon.

Beef Liege

1½ lb lean beef cut into cubes
2 oz beef dripping
4 oz mushrooms, sliced
4 oz prunes (soak overnight)
1 clove garlic, crushed
1 small bottle beer
Bouquet garni

3 onions, sliced
3 carrots, sliced
2 teaspoonsful tomato purée
1 tablespoonful plain flour
1 pint stock
Salt and freshly ground black
  pepper

Method. Heat dripping in thick pan, fry meat until brown all over, remove from fat and place in a casserole with the prunes. Fry the vegetables gently until golden, remove from fat and add them to the meat. Put flour in pan with fat, mix well and then add all the other ingredients, simmer until thick. Strain over the meat and vegetables and cook for 1½ to 2 hours in moderate oven with lid tight on casserole.

Apricot Ambrosia

Method. Simmer the contents of a medium sized tin of apricots in a small amount of the syrup until soft, then put through a sieve or blender and leave to get cold.

Whip ½ pint double cream with a tablespoonful of sugar until thick. Crumble 4 macaroon biscuits and fold them into the cream, then add the apricot purée.

Pile high into a dish and sprinkle over with flaked almonds. If desired, 2 tablespoonsful Apricot Brandy can be added to cream whilst being whipped.

Margery E. Rew

Little Woodwater, Woodwater Lane, Exeter.
Member of the Soroptimist Club of Exeter.

This favourite recipe is easy to prepare.

Sweet and Sour Pork

4 spare rib pork chops
1 oz seasoned flour
1 tablespoonful brown sugar
2 tablespoonsful vinegar
2 tablespoonsful lemon juice

1 tablespoonful flour
1 dessertspoonful dry mustard
2 oz raisins
¾ pint stock or water

Method. Brown chops on both sides in hot oil and transfer to casserole. Blend flour into fat in pan and make up with stock, stirring until smooth. Mix together the sugar, vinegar, lemon juice, mustard and add to stock. Pour this sauce over the chops and add the raisins: cover the casserole and cook 1¼ hours at gas mark 4 or 350°F. Serve with boiled rice and green salad.

Mrs J. I. Richardson

Alphington, Exeter.

Mrs Richardson is Chairman of the South West Region of the National Council of Women and President of the Exeter branch. She is also a practical worker for hospital welfare.

Devon Cider Cake

4 oz butter
4 oz sugar
2 eggs
8 oz flour (sifted)

1 teaspoonful bicarbonate of soda
½ nutmeg (well grated)
1 teacup cider

Method. Cream butter and sugar. Add eggs, well beaten. Sift in 4 oz flour and bi-carbonate of soda and grated nutmeg. Beat cider to a froth. Pour over the ingredients already mixed. Mix well. Fold in 4 oz flour and mix again. Bake in a shallow, greased tin for 45 minutes, 350°F, gas 4.

My family finds this a delicious cake.

Mrs W. H. Riches

Chairman of Exeter Y.W.C.A.

Melon, Cucumber and Tomato Salad

1 melon (canteloupe)
1 cucumber
Fresh herbs

1 lb tomatoes
French dressing

Method. Cut melon into portions and scrape out flesh. Skin and quarter tomatoes and remove seeds. Cut cucumber into cubes and sprinkle lightly with salt. Stand for ½ hour and drain off liquid. Mix fruits together, moisten with dressing to which has been added plenty of fresh herbs. Chill and serve in melon slices as a starter with brown bread and butter.

Sardine-stuffed Lemons

6 large fresh lemons
5 oz butter or home-made mayonnaise
1 egg white stiffly beaten
1 sprig fresh thyme, bay leaf or fresh green leaf per lemon

1 can sardines or tuna fish
Paprika, freshly ground black pepper and Dijon mustard

Method. Cut tops off lemons and dig out pulp with small spoon. Remove pips and reserve pulp and juice.

Mash sardines or tuna fish to a smooth paste with butter and season with paprika, black pepper and mustard. Stir in juice and pulp of lemons together with stiffly beaten egg white.

Correct seasoning and stuff lemons with this mixture and chill. Top with a sprig of fresh thyme, a bay leaf or a small green leaf. Serve in egg cups. Enough for 6.

Felicity Riches

Felicity Riches runs an 'outside catering' business, covering Cordon Bleu cuisine and picnic hampers for such activities as point-to-point meetings, etc.

Quick Steak Riches

1 lb grilling steak
4 oz mushrooms (sliced)
1 lb tomatoes (concassed)
Salt and pepper

1 large onion (sliced)
2 green peppers (sliced)
2 cloves garlic

Method. Cut steak into strips and fry in butter until cooked. Take out of pan. Fry sliced onion and mushrooms in the pan until tender, add sliced green peppers and, when cooked, return meat to pan. Season, add crushed cloves of garlic and, lastly, tomatoes.

Cook for a few more minutes and serve.

Super served with just salad.

Rum Ginger

1 packet ginger nuts
¼ pint double cream
Grated chocolate to decorate

1 measure rum
Glacé cherries

Method. Whip cream. Dip biscuits in rum and sandwich together with cream to form log shape. Mask with remaining whipped cream, grate chocolate over and decorate with cherries. Better made the day before needed. Enough for four.

Mrs A. Robb

Topsham Road, Exeter.

Ex Vice-President and ex Chairman, Exeter Branch, Y.W.C.A.

Old Priory Biscuits

2 oz margarine
2 oz rolled oats
Pinch of salt
1 dessertspoonful water

2 oz sugar
2 oz S.R. flour
1 teaspoonful golden syrup
½ level teaspoonful bi-carbonate of
soda

Method. (1) Cream fat and sugar.
(2) Mix in oats, flour and salt.
(3) Boil water and syrup, stir in soda and mix with dry ingredients.
(4) Divide into 16 balls, set far apart on baking tin.
(5) Bake 10 minutes, gas 5, 375°F.

Miss Janet Robb

Principal Nursing Officer, Devon County.

Miracle Pudding—*Serves 5 or 6. Very good!*

2 oz butter or margarine	2 teacupsful milk
2 oz Plain flour	8 oz sugar
4 eggs	2 lemons

Method. (1) Beat fat and sugar together thoroughly with 2 tablespoonsful of hot water.

(2) Stir in sifted flour, grated rind and juice of lemons, yolks of eggs and milk.

(3) Mix with rotary whisk.

(4) Fold in stiffly beaten whites of eggs.

(5) Pour into buttered pie dish and bake in a slow oven, gas 3 or 325°F, for 1½ hours.

Dr G. H. Robb

Eggs in Purgatory

Method. For every 2 eggs cook in a flat pan 2–3 peeled tomatoes (fresh or tinned) in 1 tablespoonful olive oil until they make a purée. Break eggs into mixture and spoon some over them, being careful not to break the yolks. Season and serve on buttered toast.

Mrs Brenda Robinson

'One of the girls in the newsroom at B.B.C. Plymouth.'

Brenda's Biscuits

2 handfuls crushed cornflakes	1 cup coconut
½ cup brown sugar	1 cup S.R. flour
4 oz butter or margarine	2 dessertspoonsful drinking chocolate (if liked)

Method. Melt butter and add to dry ingredients, which should have been well mixed through. Press into slab tin (approx. 14 in. by 8 in.), and cook in a moderate oven for about 10–15 minutes. Ice while still hot with chocolate icing. Cut when cold.

Very approximate measures for icing—6 oz icing sugar, 2 heaped teaspoonsful cocoa, well sieved together and sufficient warm water to make a stiff spreading consistency.

The Lady Roborough

Roborough, Plymouth.

Wife of the Lord Lieutenant of the County of Devon.

I enclose a recipe easy to do, if one is cooking for oneself for a party, and one I have never seen in a book.

½ lb puff pastry
6 tablespoonsful sherry

4 oz apricot jam
¾ pint double cream

Method. Roll out the pastry very thin and cut into strips about 6 in. by 3 in. Place on a baking sheet and prick with a fork. Cook until golden brown and leave to get cold.

Mix jam and sherry together, take half the cream and whisk until quite thick. Spread a layer of jam mixture and then a layer of thickened cream on top of the cooked pastry strips and pile one on top of the other, that is, pastry, filling, pastry, filling then pastry again and then pour over the rest of the double cream and serve at once.

Miss C. M. Ross, M.B.E.

Member of Exeter City Council and member of Housing, Education and Children's Committees. Member of Exe Vale Hospitals Management Committee. Member of War Pensioners' Welfare Service.

'In private life I am a grocer in partnership with two ex-service friends. From a beginning in a converted, war-time ambulance, serving tea, etc. on Paul Street Coach Park, we now own and manage one of Exeter's biggest independent Supermarkets'.

Burnt Grapes

1 lb grapes
½ pint double cream

6 oz brown sugar

This is a delicious dinner party sweet which can be prepared and refrigerated until required.

Method. Peel and de-pip grapes. Place in a shallow fire-proof dish, pour over the cream. Sprinkle sugar on top. When ready to serve, place under a red hot grill for five minutes.

Exeter Sandwich—*This is an Exeter recipe at least 200 years old.*

8 oz flour
4 oz caster sugar
Raspberry jam

4 oz butter
1 beaten egg
2–3 oz whole almonds split in
    halves and skinned

Method. Rub butter into flour, add sugar, mix in beaten egg. Knead lightly and halve mixture. Roll out one half to fit 7 inch sandwich tin. Press in, spread generously with raspberry jam. Cover with second half pressing edges together to seal in the jam. Cover top with halved skinned almonds. Cook middle shelf, 40 minutes. Reg. 5, 375°F. Serve cold.

Isabel Ross

formerly Warden of Lopes Hall, University of Exeter.

Household Broth

This excellent broth is even acceptable to Scots, and although the careful washing and preparation of the vegetables take time, the result is rewarding and satisfying, specially on a winter's day.

2 lb rolled brisket of beef	5 pints boiling water
½ teacup barley	⅓ teacup lentils
3 leeks	Small piece turnip
6 or so brussels sprouts	3 small onions
1 small carrot	Some green peas
A few chives	Small quantity parsley

Method. Place brisket of beef in boiling water in soup pan. Add ½ teacup barley, which has been washed through with water in a fine sieve. Next add lentils, washed in same manner. Stir occasionally. Add diced vegetables, except brussels sprouts. The brussels sprouts are finely shredded and added fully twenty minutes before serving. The leeks, leafy green parts as well, can be cut up with scissors. Season with salt, about ½ to ¾ of a dessertspoonful, not too much salt. Boil slowly on a low gas for 2½ hours, stirring the soup at intervals, and watching lest it boil over the pan. Add a little boiling water if the broth becomes too thick.

Chives and parsley are added last of all—sprinkled on to the broth shortly before it is to be served.

The meat is not very exciting to eat, but can be served sliced with potatoes. If the broth is used for a second time it must be thoroughly re-boiled. Water should be added if it is used again. The amounts stated should make enough broth for four or five people, and beef makes much better broth than mutton, because it is less greasy.

———❖　❖　❖———

The meaning of 'Devon'.
'. . . the name of Devon is derived ultimately from a Celtic tribal name—"the people of the land". Both the modern forms Devon and Devonshire—are equally ancient, dating from the earliest days of the shire in the ninth century. Neither usage is more correct than the other. The form we use to-day is governed largely by the euphony required in a phrase and partly by custom. Thus we speak of Red Devon Cattle, and we used to speak of Devonshire Cream.'

Devon, PROFESSOR W. G. HOSKINS.

Marian Ross

wife of the Secretary of the University of Exeter.

Apricot Flan

Pastry:

5 oz flour
2½ oz margarine
1 oz caster sugar
1 egg yolk
2 oz cake crumbs

Filling:

2 oz caster sugar
1 gill double cream
1 egg yolk
1 large tin apricots (drained)

Glaze:

2 tablespoons sieved apricot jam   Juice ½ lemon

Method. (1) Flan pastry. Rub fat into flour, add sugar and egg yolk and mix, adding a very little water only if necessary. Roll out to fit 8–9 inch flan ring or sponge sandwich tin. Bake 12 minutes at 400°F, gas 6.

(2) Filling. Beat sugar and egg yolk into cream.

(3) Cover base of flan with cake crumbs.

(4) Arrange apricots, hollow side down, on crumbs. Cover with cream mixture. Replace in moderate oven for 15 minutes, 350°F, gas 4.

(5) Boil sieved apricot jam and lemon juice. Cover the flan with this glaze, and allow to cool.

Mrs John Rossiter

Muriel Rossiter won the Junket Championship in 1935; 'Western Morning News' Challenge Cup for Churn Buttermaking in 1936 and 1937; Royal London Dairy Show, First in 1935, 1936 and 1937 for Fancy Butter and Floral Arrangement in Butter. Married in 1938 to John Rossiter, breeder of the 'Cholwells' herd of South Devons, first registered in 1918. Farming in the Kingsbridge area of the South Hams.

Squab Pie (*i.e. 'Squabble Pie—the compromise—the master demanding meat pie and the mistress wanting apple'*).

Breast of lamb
4–5 apples
2 oz sugar

Short or rough puff pastry
2 large onions
Seasoning

Method. Boil lamb in seasoned water until tender. When cold, remove bone and excess fat, chop into small cubes, slice apples and onions. Into a pie dish place alternate layers (thin) of onion, lamb, apple and sugar, seasoning to taste. Add about 1 cup stock. Cover with a lid of pastry, bake until apple and onion are cooked. Thicken remainder of stock, colour and use as gravy.

Concise Oxford Dictionary gives 'Squab—short and fat, squat—pigeon pie or pie made of mutton, apples and onions; a stuffed cushion, etc.'

Roma Rowe

Clyst St. Mary, Near Exeter.

Mrs Rowe is the wife of the Chairman of the Exeter Y.W.C.A.
Development Committee.

Christmas Pudding—*A delicious old and tried recipe; two small puddings were sent to the Antarctic where our son had been with the British Antarctic Survey October 1967–1970.*

1 glass brandy (sherry glass size)	½ teaspoonful each of mixed spice
4 oz plain flour	Grated nutmeg
1 lb stoned prunes	Salt
1 lb shredded beef suet	1 apple (finely chopped)
1 lb stoned raisins	4 oz mixed peel
1 lb currants	2 oz sweet almonds
Juice of lemon and finely grated rind	6 eggs

Method. Mix all dry ingredients. Beat eggs. Add all chopped fruits and nuts to flour. Make a well in centre of ingredients and gradually add eggs, stirring very well all the time. Finally add lemon juice and brandy. Keep stirring till all is very thoroughly mixed. Butter two large pudding bowls, fill and tie first with greaseproof greased paper, then with cloth. Steam 10 hours. Put clean cloths on when cold. Steam 2 hours on day required.

---- ✦ ✦ ✦ ----

Note to trading Captain at end of sixteenth century.—Richard Hayklutt 1553–1616.
Banketting on shipboard of persons of credite.

First the sweetest perfumes to set under hatches to make ye place sweet against their coming aboord.

Marmelade	(Figs barrelled)
Sucket	(Raisins of the sunne)

Comfets of divers kinds made of purpose by him, that is most excellent, that shall not dissolve.

Prunes Damaske	(Walnuts)
Dried peares	(Almonds)

Olives to make them taste their wine.

The apple John, that dureth two yeeres, to make shew of our fruits.

Hullocke	(Sacke)

Vials of good sweet waters, and casting bottels of glasses to bespringkle the guests withall, after their coming aboard.

Sugar to use with their wine if they will.

Excellent French vinegar, and a fine kind of Bisket stieped in the same do make a banketting dish, and a little sugar cast in it cooleth and comforteth and refresheth the spirits of man.

Cynamon water, Imperial water, is to be had with you to make a shew of by taste, and also to comfort your sick in the voyage.

With these and suchlike, you may banket where you arrive the greater and best persons.

Or with the gift of these Marmelades in small boxes, or small vials of sweet waters you may gratifie by way of gift, or you may make a merchandize of them.

Hilda Rowe

Countess Wear, Exeter.

Cheese Scones

5 oz self raising flour
A little milk to mix
¼ teaspoonful dry mustard

1 oz butter or margarine
5 oz grated cheese
Pinch of salt

Method. Mix together flour, cheese, mustard, salt. Rub in butter and mix to a soft dough with a little milk. Cut in 2 inch rounds. Bake in centre of oven, Reg. 8 (450°F) for 8 minutes.

Jennifer Rowland

Exeter Ladies' Circle.

Chocolate Biscuit Cake

4 oz butter
2 tablespoonsful cocoa
Bournville chocolate 4 oz

2 tablespoonsful Golden Syrup
1 packet Digestive biscuits
4 tablespoonsful icing sugar

Method. Melt butter and syrup over low heat. Add cocoa. Crush biscuits and add. Put into shallow dish and press down. Melt chocolate over boiling water and add icing sugar and a little water to moisten. Spread over chocolate cake and put in refrigerator for 4 hours.

Miss O. M. Rudd, O.B.E., J.P.

20, Riverside Road, Topsham, Exeter, Devon.
Governor: Bishop Blackall School, Exeter.
Trustee: Woodhayes Eventide Home, Exeter.

Apple and Blackberry Chutney

1½ lb apples (after peeling and coring)
½ pint vinegar
¼ lb brown sugar
1 teaspoonful salt
1 teaspoonful cayenne pepper
1 teaspoonful ground ginger

1½ lb blackberries
4 oz each raisins (stoned and
    chopped) and sultanas
2 cloves of garlic (or 3 small
    onions, finely chopped)

Method. Prepare ingredients, other than the blackberries. Wash the berries and put them in a pan with the vinegar. Crush well with a wooden masher. Simmer together for about 20 minutes then rub through a sieve. Add the remaining ingredients, stir well to dissolve the sugar, then cook gently until the mixture is thick—about 40 minutes. If garlic has been used, remove after cooking. Put chutney into warm jars, filling well, and cover down firmly.

90

E. Sacco

Chef de Cuisine, Rougemont Hotel, Exeter

MENU FOR FOUR

Gnocchi a la Romaina

1 pint milk
Parmesan cheese
Nutmeg
2 egg yolks

4 oz semolina
Pinch of salt
Butter

Method. Bring milk to boil, add semolina, salt and nutmeg to taste. Cook for 5–6 minutes. Remove from heat, add egg yolks and beat. Pour into large flat dish and spread to a depth of ½ inch. When cold, cut into discs. Place in casserole with Parmesan cheese, dot with butter. Place in hot oven until brown.

Paillarde a la Pizzaiola

4 slices of Devon sirloin of beef *or*
   4 escalopes of veal
1 clove garlic
1 onion (sliced)

4–5 fresh peeled tomatoes
Flour, seasoned
1 glass white wine

Method. Flatten meat as much as possible then coat in flour. Melt butter and fry meat for about 5–6 minutes (or until tender). Remove from pan. Place onion and finely chopped garlic in pan, fry until golden. Add chopped tomatoes and cook for 5–6 minutes. Then replace escalopes, bring to boil and serve.

Patate Macario

4–5 large potatoes

Milk and butter

Method. Peel potatoes, boil in slightly salted water. Mash with a little milk and butter. Place in casserole dish, dot with butter. Place under hot grill until brown. Cut into squares and serve.

Melanzane Trifoliate

4 medium-sized aubergines (egg plant)
1 onion (sliced)
Butter

Chopped parsley
Salt and black pepper

Method. Slice aubergines, cut in small squares. Sauté onion in butter. Add chopped parsley then aubergines. Add salt and black pepper to taste.
  Aubergines successfully grow in Devon gardens.

Zabaglione

4 egg yolks
3 by ½ egg-shells Marsala or sweet
  sherry

2 tablespoonsful caster sugar
3 by ½ egg-shells white wine

Method. Put all ingredients together in the top of a double saucepan, beat over hot water until stiff. Serve with sponge fingers.

Ross Salmon

Broadcaster and Farmer.

Those who know I farm on Dartmoor, might associate me with a recipe from that area. And the other one is jolly nice.

Devon Pie

Method. (1) Line a plate with short-crust pastry (4 oz flour, 2 oz fat).

(2) For filling use 2 oz lean bacon, a small onion, an egg, 4 mushrooms, 1 oz grated cheese, 1 cup (½ pint) milk, 1 oz butter.

(3) Peel and chop onion and mushrooms; fry gently in butter; cut up the bacon, add to frying vegetables and cook gently for 10 minutes, stirring frequently.

(4) Mix egg with milk, stir the grated cheese into this, add cooked bacon, onion and mushrooms. Mix well, season lightly, then pour into the pastry case.

(5) Bake in a moderate oven (Gas 5, 375°F) about 25 minutes until the filling has set. Serve hot or cold.

'Dartmoor Ducks'

Method. A quick supper or lunch dish. It's a pound of pork sausages with a little dry sage and onion stuffing, covered with a layer of tomatoes (fresh or tinned) and a thick layer of cooked haricot beans. Cook slowly in a covered pan. Serve with mashed potatoes.

Saltram House
Near Plymouth.

Saltram House is a National Trust property; it is a George II mansion, embodying the remains of a Tudor and late Stuart House. In the middle of the eighteenth century the house was altered and added to. But the kitchens were not changed, and the Tudor Great Kitchen remains; the principal feature is the collection of 600 pieces of copper tinned internally, about half of which was found hidden away in a cupboard at the back of the house; numerous moulds for jellies and ices remain. We have been given permission by the National Trust to reproduce these recipes from Saltram.

Sullebubbles (A.D. 1600)

Method. Take a pint of good cream, and half a pint of fresh rich milk, and put them into a dry pan, and put therein a spoonful of orange flower water and a little white wine. Sweeten with fine sugar. Beat the whites of 2 eggs, and put them in. Take the mill (nowadays an egg whisk or rotary beater) and grind well, take off the froth with a spoon, and put it in your glasses as high as you can. If you will have it of a red colour, put in clarett instead of white wine, and a little in the bottom of the glass with a little sugar.

A Goodlie Pye (A.D. 1600)

Method. Take small chickeyens . . . make of pastrie the best. Then lay the chickeyns side by side on the pastrie after filling their bellies full of bredcrumbs mixed with fresh butter, parsley, thyme pepper and salt, wrap pastrie over them, wetting and moulding the edges together. Bake in a Dutch oven before the fire, turning occasionally, till pastrie is golden, then serve in a deep oval dish, and hand round this Egg and Wine Sauce, in a sauceboat along it: Mix 6 beaten egg yolks with white wine, vinegar, pepper, salt and ground cinnamon, sugar and rosewater to taste, and cook till sauce thickens.

If a Dutch oven is no longer in use . . . '. . . bake as you would chicken pie in a hot oven, 475°F, gas 9, till pastry is risen and set, then lower to fairly slow, 325°F, gas 3, and finish cooking. It would be wise to cook sauce in a double boiler. Be sure to stir constantly, and be careful not to add more than a drop or two of rosewater, 1 knob of sugar and a tiny pinch of cinnamon . . .'. *These recipes have been tested and the notes kindly added by the Plymouth College of Domestic Science.*

Lady Sayer

Widecombe-in-the-Moor.

Mousse au Chocolat Basque—For 8 people.

Approximate time to prepare 10 minutes.

½ lb sweetened chocolate   1 dessertspoonful rum
1 teaspoonful oil, or nut of butter   ½ gill cold water
5 eggs

Method.   Mousse. Cut the chocolate up finely, put into a pan with the water and oil. Stir over a slow fire and achieve smoothness. Remove, cool, add the rum, and beat in the five yolks of egg. Lastly, add the five stiffly whipped whites of egg, and beat 5–6 minutes.

Setting and serving. Pour into small earthenware pots and set in a cool place for at least six hours before serving. They are better made the day before.

Vice-Admiral Sir Guy Sayer, M.B.E., C.B., D.S.C., Cator, Widecombe-in-the-Moor, Devon, sent this recipe, and was able personally to testify to its deliciousness. 'My wife was born in Plymouth in 1904, the daughter of Surgeon Captain and Mrs R. C. Munday. Married in 1925, we have twin sons, both married, and three granddaughters. Her maternal great grandfather—Charles Burnard—was Mayor of Plymouth, and a founder member of the Dartmoor Preservation Association, of which my wife has been Chairman since 1952.

Her maternal grandfather, Robert Burnard, was Hon. Sec. of D.P.A. and a very prominent figure in the preservation of Dartmoor. He lived for many years at Huccaby House, Hexworthy, where my wife spent much time as a child, and gained the deep love of the Moor which is so much part of her being today.

We have had our home at Cator, Widecombe-in-the-Moor, since 1928.

My wife has served on various public and other bodies, e.g. Newton Abbot Rural District Council, (member for Widecombe), Widecombe Parish Council, Minister's nominee on Dartmoor National Park Committee of Devon County Council, Vice-President of Ramblers Association of Great Britain, Standing Committee on National Parks of the C.P.R.E., Committee of the Commons, Footpaths, and Open Spaces Preservation Society, etc.'

——— ❖ ❖ ❖ ———

'The sun was already sinking when I reached the summit of the hill, and the long slopes beneath me were all golden green on one side and grey shadow on the other. A haze lay low upon the farthest sky-line, out of which jutted the fantastic shapes of Bellever and Vixen Tor. Over the wide expanse there was no sound and no movement. One great grey bird, a gull or curlew, soared aloft in the blue heaven. He and I seemed to be the only living things between the huge arch of the sky and the desert beneath it.'

The Hound of the Baskervilles—SIR ARTHUR CONAN DOYLE.

Margery, Lady Sebright

Topsham.

Salad Isabella

1 lb cooked cold chicken	½ pint mayonnaise
1 teaspoonful paprika	3 oz cooked Patna rice
Seasonings	A few cooked or canned
Sliced tomatoes added for colour	asparagus tips

Method. (1) Dice or slice chicken into small pieces.
    (2) Blend with mayonnaise, paprika, rice and add seasoning to taste.
    (3) Pile on to bed of lettuce and garnish with asparagus tips.

Doris Sharland

Exeter.

Member of Soroptimist Club of Exeter.

Coffee Pudding (no cooking).

Make overnight.

2 eggs	4 oz caster sugar
4 oz butter	2 tablespoonsful Camp coffee or
5 sponge cakes	similar
1 wineglass of sherry and water mixed	¼ pint whipped cream

Method. Beat butter and sugar together, beat in eggs (don't worry if it curdles slightly), add coffee. Cut sponge cakes into three slices each, then into six 'fingers' and line sides and bottom of a 1 pint basin. Moisten with sherry and water. Gently pour in the coffee mixture. Leave to set overnight, turn out and cover with whipped cream. Garnish with grated chocolate.

'The oldest and perhaps the most interesting of the hostelries is the Bridge Inn, on the banks of the River Clyst. It has an ancient history, being first mentioned in Domesday Book as a lodging house for some of the stone masons who were helping to build Exeter Cathedral. In the seventeenth century a man named Meekin lived there owning a salt factory . . . he made a large fortune. Mr Gibbings the present landlord, remembers . . . a huge block of rock salt was found, embedded in the earth . . . the remains of a landing stage, or wharf, on the river bank . . . where the rock salt was landed. A part of an old rusty knife was also found at the time of the excavations . . . archaeologists are of the opinion that it is Roman; . . . hiding holes . . . give evidence that the inn was the headquarters of smugglers in Elizabethan times; . . . A large Hall, . . . and much of its original Cornish clay floor is intact. Brewing took place on the premises as lately as 1878, when the great fire in its massive round chimney was lit for the last time.'

The Story of the Manor and Port of Topsham—D. M. BRADBEER.

Mrs G. Shepherd

Matford Avenue, Exeter.

Mr Shepherd is a Director of Grays of Exeter.

'*This is a favourite recipe but not strictly traditionally Devonshire.*'

Braised Topside—Serves 6.

2 lb topside beef
3 onions
2 strips lemon peel
1 bay leaf
1 beef stock cube
¾ pint water
1 clove garlic if liked (crushed)

5 tablespoonsful corn oil
1 gill red wine
3 oz chopped bacon
2 tablespoonsful cornflour
Salt, pepper, thyme, rosemary,
    parsley stalk

Method. Cut the meat into fairly large slices and put into dish. Sprinkle with pepper and salt. Cover with sliced onion, bay leaf, lemon peel. Pour the red wine and 2 tablespoonsful corn oil over meat and leave to marinade for a few hours.

Heat 3 tablespoonsful oil in large pan or casserole which can be used on top of the cooker. Add bacon and remaining sliced onions and cook until lightly browned. Remove meat from marinade, drain well, coat with cornflour and brown in the oil. Add strained marinade, crumbled beef cube, water, herbs and garlic. Bring to the point of boiling, cover and simmer for 2 hours or until meat is tender. Correct seasoning and remove bouquet garni before serving.

R. J. Smerdon

Exeter.

This dish was first demonstrated at an Arts Festival at Tiverton Grammar School, Devon, and Mr Smerdon named it in his wife's memory. Mr John Smerdon is well known in the field of Catering. He is a Lecturer in Food and Beverage Preparation and Service at the Exeter Technical College. He gives extra-mural lectures and demonstrations to many groups and societies in the County, and as far as he is aware, his work at the Exeter Prison, training men for Waiters' positions, is the only course of its kind in the country, and indeed, in the world.

Entrecote Diane Elizabeth

2 sirloin steaks (4–6 oz) Devon beef
1 lb stoned cherries
Cognac
Salt and pepper

4 oz butter
1 finely chopped small onion
2 gills Double Devon cream

Method. (1) Ensure that the steaks are well-flattened.

(2) Season with salt and pepper

(3) Sauté the steaks in the melted butter.

(4) When cooked, remove and keep hot.

(5) Sauté the onions and as they begin to take colour, add the stoned cherries.

(6) Return the steaks to the pan.

(7) Flame with the cognac.

(8) Pour over the cream, heat and serve.

(9) Serve with pommes Pont Neuf and green salad.

Pommes Pont Neuf

Method. Scrub and peel even-sized potatoes, cut and trim into pieces just under 1 in. by 1 in. by 2 in. Wash, and dry on a cloth. Cook in moderately hot fat without colouring the potatoes. Drain. Re-heat fat until almost smoking, re-cook potatoes until golden brown, drain, and season with salt.

Syllabub—*to accompany fresh strawberries.*

½ pint double cream
Little icing sugar
Strained juice of 1 orange

1 wineglass Chablis
Finely grated rind of an orange

Method. Beat all together for a few minutes until light.

H. N. Snowdon

Clanacombe Farm, Kingsbridge.

Mr Snowdon is a farmer with a lifelong interest in natural history, particularly bird watching. His hobbies are painting, oil and water colour, but some of his most pleasant pictures are pastels. He is interested in wood-turning and writing.

To skin rabbit (or hare)

Starting along the slit from where the paunch has been removed, separate with the fingers, the skin from the flesh, working round the back and towards the back legs. Push each back leg out of the skin, and cut off feet. Finish back end by pulling skin off at tail.

Next pull skin down over front and removing front legs as before, and finish by cutting head off at neck. If skin is of value for curing, remove head and feet, and spread pelt on board to dry.

To joint rabbit, cut off legs at joints close to body, cut body into three. *Suggested recipes.* Adult rabbit, roast with sage and onions and fat bacon. Young rabbit, bake in pie with parsley and bacon. Either recipe can be served hot or cold.

To pluck a chicken or pheasant

Starting at the neck pluck off cleanly breast feathers, each wing, back, each leg and finish at tail.

To avoid tough wing feathers, cut off end joint (no one eats it).

To avoid stripping skin take very few feathers at a time and pull carefully. Speed comes with practice. Areas most likely to strip are the rough patches of skin each side of the breast, and on thighs. Observe those on plucked chicken.

Alternative method—hang chicken up by one leg and pluck from top downwards, over a bin.

To dress chicken

Cut off feet and shank of legs. Cut skin right round neck about an inch from body. Remove neck by drawing skin back either way and cutting off head, then neck, from close to body.

Remove crop (food sack attached under skin in neck cavity).

Singe any hair off chicken with taper. Insert forefinger through neck cavity and loosen any membrane attached to breast cavity as far as can be reached. Next carefully slice across abdomen between vent and end of breast-bone. Insert hand along under breast over gizzard, well forward over heart and liver, withdraw whole of entrails, which should detach from the back. Cut around vent for final separation. Remove lungs if still attached, check cavity is clear, and wash through. *Giblets.* Cut away liver taking care not to break green gall bladder. Cut gizzard away from entrails and carefully slice across to expose inner grit sack, which if not cut can be peeled clearly away from fleshy part. Include neck and heart with giblets.

Suggested recipes. Chicken. Stuff with parsley and thyme, roast and serve with roast pork and crackling.

Hen. Fowl pie. Joint bird and bake in a pie with fat bacon and parsley chopped.

Tony Soper

Salter Mill, Landulph, Saltash, Cornwall.

Tony Soper considers himself not the best cook in Devon, but he likes his food nevertheless. Although his Corned Gulls Eggs is perhaps his best achievement so far, he also has a hot line in mackerel cooked in a bucket of sea water and in scallops cooked on a driftwood fire. Aside from his culinary activities, he is a naturalist, working as a writer and freelance broadcaster.

Corned Gulls' Eggs

Method. Take 3 Herring Gull eggs (collected on the Devon cliffs in May). Make sure they're new-laid, i.e. take them from nests where only one egg of the clutch has been laid or you'll get a surprise when you crack them open. (N.B. Herring Gulls are too numerous, so taking the eggs is the act of a good conservationist.) Take 1 can of Argentinian corned beef. Pat of butter. Any other food that's available.

Climb down to the beach and light a small driftwood fire. Leave the ingredients somewhere where the dog can't get at them and go and have a swim. By the time you get back the fire will consist of red-hot embers. Melt the pat of butter in a frying pan. Add the corned beef and anything else. After five minutes put the eggs in. Don't be alarmed when the 'white' doesn't turn white. When the yellow part looks as if it's cooked, take a clean stick, or the wrong end of a biro pen and stir the whole thing well for a couple of minutes. Eat it from the pan. (There should be enough for two, but it all depends.)

The Hon. Mrs J. E. Stannard

Kingswear.

President West Country Crafts Stall, Y.W.C.A. National Christmas Fair.

Apricot Pork Chops—For 6 people.

6 pork loin chops	2 tablespoonsful tomato purée
1 oz butter	Grated rind of 1 orange
1 onion	2 bay leaves
½ oz flour	3–4 tablespoonsful vinegar
1 medium can halved apricots	

Method. 1. Trim chops and remove rind.

2. Fry in butter until just brown.

3. Place in shallow casserole.

4. Chop onion and fry in fat left in pan.

5. Stir in flour, cook for several minutes. Remove from heat.

6. Reserve 6 apricots for garnish, sieve or liquidise rest to form purée.

7. Stir into pan with tomato purée, orange rind, bay leaves, vinegar, seasoning to taste.

8. Bring to boil stirring, cook 1–2 minutes.

9. Pour over chops, cover, cook in oven, gas 6, 400°F.

10. Remove pith from orange and slice.

11. Lift chops from casserole on to hot dish.

12. Garnish with orange slices and apricots.

Mr and Mrs M. W. Stock

Bishopsteignton, South Devon.

Mr Stock is Devon County Dairy Husbandry Adviser.

Woodpigeon Recipes

(Ringdove, cusha or queest) Columba Palumbus

These are excellent in whatever way cooked, but there is little meat except on the breast. To save plucking and cleaning merely skin the breast and fillet the meat off, in two steaks of about 2 oz each. These can be stored in refrigerator or freezer for use as required.

Palumbus Steaks

Breasts of 6 pigeons
2 level tablespoons plain flour (approx.)
2 sticks celery (if available)
1 oz butter
½ pint stock, or if necessary a beef cube

Salt and pepper
1½ lb tomatoes
1 good sized onion
1 tablespoonful Worcester sauce

Method. Put the flour in a plastic bag, add pepper and salt and shake up. Add the washed and dried breasts of pigeons and shake again. (This is a quick way of coating any meat).

Skin the tomatoes by immersing in boiling water, then in cold, when the skins will slip off easily.

Cut up finely both the onion and celery.

Fry onion gently in the butter until slightly browned. Add breasts to pan and brown on both sides. Add the Worcester sauce and the stock and bring to the boil, stirring all the time.

Place in a casserole, adding tomatoes and chopped celery.

Cover and cook in a moderate oven for about 2 hours, 300°F, gas 2.

Game Preserve

Method. Simmer any number of prepared pigeons for about 3 hours or more. Add to this during the cooking period, an onion, 6 peppercorns, sprig parsley and thyme.

When cooked allow to cool. Take meat off bones and chop up with a sharp knife, putting chopped meat in a big bowl. Add pepper and salt. Add gelatine, ½ oz to about ½ pint of the stock in which birds were cooked, and when dissolved, cool and add to the meat, mixing thoroughly. Put in basins or other containers, smooth the tops, and place in refrigerator, or cool place to set. Turn out and serve with salad. It is excellent sliced for sandwiches.

Melon
Casseroled chicken
Fresh fruit salad, Devonshire cream
Biscuits, Devon butter and cheese

Melon

Method. Cut generous slices from the melon, remove pips. Using a sharp knife cut between flesh and skin: cut the flesh across in slices, and pull the slices in alternate directions. I think the flavour is better at room temperature, so chill only in very hot weather. Serve with caster sugar and ground ginger if liked.

Casseroled Chicken

1 chicken	2 oz butter
1 onion	1 lb carrots
Sprig thyme	4 oz button mushrooms
¾ pint stock, chicken or made with cube	Fresh or frozen peas
Potatoes	

Method. Joint the chicken, wash and dry well. Fry in the butter until brown on all sides.

Put in large casserole with mushrooms and thyme. Slice onion thinly and scrape about 3 of the carrots and cut into strips. Fry in butter after the chicken. Put in casserole. Add stock. Cover, and cook for 1½ hours, 350°F, gas 4.

Serve with peas, remainder of the carrots (tossed in butter after cooking) and mashed potatoes.

Fresh Fruit Salad

Any kind of fresh fruit, grapes, apple, pear, peach, apricot, orange, ½ grapefruit, 2 bananas

4 oz sugar   ½ pint water

Method. Dissolve sugar in boiling water and boil 2 minutes. Allow to cool, Add 1 tablespoonful Cointreau or Cherry Brandy to the syrup when cool (*for special occasions, e.g. our Wedding Anniversary*). Wash grapes, peel and remove pips. Slice bananas. Peel apple and pear, peach and apricot. If necessary dip latter two in hot water for a minute or two to remove skin. Peel orange and cut into thin round slices. Peel grapefruit and remove skin from each segment. Arrange all fruit in bowl and pour syrup over. Cover and allow to stand for at least 2 hours. Serve with cream.

Lady Studholme

Wembury, Plymouth.

Avocado Pears and Shrimps

To 1 pear, ½ cup of shrimps

Method. Cut pear in half and scoop out flesh into a basin. Mash roughly with a fork, mix in ½ teaspoonful of olive oil and ½ teaspoonful of vinegar, salt and pepper, mix in shrimps. Put into refrigerator and leave till ½ hour before serving. Mix in 2 tablespoonsful thick cream. Mix well, put into pear shells and serve.

Douglas J. Sutherland

Head of Department of Catering, North Devon Technical College, Barnstaple.

Mr Sutherland came to Devon six years ago, to a newly-created appointment. He has won over 200 Premier awards in International Culinary Exhibitions. Serves on the senior panel of judges at Hotelympia and other major exhibitions. His career has followed the classical tradition, working in some of the country's most famous hotels, Gleneagles, Grosvenor House, Park Lane, etc. He is now happily settled in Devon, and is very proud of the achievements of his students who have completed their training under his tuition, and are now working in senior posts both here and abroad.

Galette Montmorency—Cherry Cake

Galette Paste:

16 oz flour	4 oz icing sugar
10 oz butter	4 egg yolks (approx.)
1–2 drops vanilla essence	

N.B. 2 oz of the flour may be replaced by 2 oz ground almonds, which will enhance the finished flavour.

Method. Cream the fat, sugar, and egg yolks, and add vanilla. Shake in flour, and lightly rub down to a smooth paste. Allow to rest in a cool place before rolling out to ⅜ inch thickness. Mark a circle approximately 8 inches diameter. Cut out, place on silicone paper lined baking sheet. Bake at 425°F, gas 7, to a pale golden brown.

Filling. Layer with stoned cherries, glaze with boiling red–currant jelly. Allow to cool. Pipe up border with whipped cream.

Edible Crystallized and Frosted Flowers, Fruit and Leaves

Crystallizing. Mix 3 teaspoonsful of fine gum arabic (Acacia No. 1), with 3 tablespoonsful triple strength rose water, or orange flower water.

Method. Paint each freshly gathered flower or leaf with the mixture, using a fine paint brush. Coat each petal or leaf on both sides, sprinkle thoroughly with caster sugar, and place on a wire tray to dry in a gently warm place.

Gather flowers to be crystallized when they are dry. Violets, primroses, rose petals and polyanthus are suitable. Some flowers, and *all* flowers from bulbs, are poisonous. Mint leaves are decorative and delicious. An airtight container will keep the crystallized flowers and leaves crisp until your special occasion.

Frosted. *Method.* Take some clean bunches of grapes, or Devon peaches or pears, clusters of red and white currants, cherries, plums, or the Alpine strawberries which grow so well in Devonshire. Dip them in stiffly beaten egg white, shake caster sugar over them and put to dry. This remains sparklingly white for a few hours only.

Mint leaves can be frosted in this way; they can be put on waxed paper in a warm place, or very low oven to dry, and when perfectly dry store between waxed paper.

Candied Angelica

Gather the stalks of Angelica in April or May, when they are tender and bright green. It is not possible to candy stringy old stalks.

Method. Cut stalks into 2 or 3 inch lengths, and put into a bowl. Boil together 4 pints water and ¼ oz salt, and pour over the Angelica, leave for 10 minutes, and then rinse in cold water. Place the stalks in a saucepan, cover with freshly boiled water, and boil for 5 minutes. Drain, and scrape off the outer skin.

Add 1 pint of water to 1 lb sugar (or ½ lb sugar, ½ lb glucose), a little green colouring (from Health Food shops), if liked. Bring to the boil, and pour over the Angelica.

On each of the seven following days, strain off the syrup into a saucepan, add 2 oz sugar, bring to the boil, and return to the Angelica; the syrup should be like runny-honey. Leave the Angelica in the syrup for 2 or 3 weeks; alternatively, drain it well, and after 3 days dry it in a very cool oven. Store in screw-top jars away from the light.

A pot-pourri in a room gives a delicate fragrance, and the following is a foundation recipe, for additions as they are available.

Method. Three-quarter fill a container with heavily scented rose-petals, which should be dried away from the sun. Add a cupful of dried leaves of thyme, lemon balm, rosemary, marjoram; a few powdered bay leaves, and the dried and crushed peel of an orange, ½ oz crushed cloves and a pinch of allspice. If lemon-scented geranium and lemon peel instead of orange, are used, and less powerful rose petals, the result is more pungent.

A. Robinson Thomas, M.A., M.B.

Chevalier du Tastevin
Chevalier de l'Ordre des Côteaux (Commanderie de Champagne)
Hon. Sec. South Devon (Torbay) Branch International Wine and
Food Society.

Devonshire Scallops

Method. Cut up the scallops, having removed the black portion, butter some shells or ramikins, and put a narrow border of creamy mashed potatoes round each. Put in the scallops and cover with a thick white sauce (cream, if possible, for both sauce and mashed potato). Sprinkle with breadcrumbs and a few dabs of butter, and bake in a moderate oven for about 20 minutes.

Suggested wine: Seyssel.

Pigeonneau a la Crapaudine—Sauce diable

Allow 1 pigeon per person. Split the pigeon down the middle, along the breast bone, and flatten out.

Method. Dab a little butter on both sides and grill slowly until golden brown. Serve up on dish, garnished with sliced pickled cucumbers, add sauce diable when serving.

Suggested wine: Egri Bikaver.

Sauce diable

¾ cup of white wine   1 tablespoon vinegar
1 tablespoon chopped shallot   Sprig thyme
¼ bay leaf   Pinch fresh ground black pepper

Method. Reduce this to two-thirds by boiling, stir in 1 cup brown gravy sauce, heat up and pour without straining.

Lemon Syllabub

½ pint double cream   4 oz caster sugar
Finely grated rind and juice of 1 large 4 tablespoonsful dry sherry
    lemon   (good quality)
Glacé cherries and sugared lemon   Sponge finger biscuits for serving
    slices for decoration

Method. Measure the cream, sugar, grated lemon rind, strained lemon juice and sherry into a mixing basin. Whisk together until quite thick: this may take 2–3 minutes. Spoon or pipe (using a large nylon piping bag fitted with a rosette nozzle) into six serving glasses. Decorate with a glacé cherry and a sugared lemon slice. Chill for several hours, then serve with sponge finger biscuits.

Suggested wine: Tokay Aszu.

The Late Mrs Jeremy Thorpe

Pork Chops in Cider

4 pork chops	1½ oz butter
1 oz flour	1 teaspoonful dried rosemary
Salt and black pepper	½ pint Devon cider plus stock
	or water if needed

Method. Fry the pork chops quickly on both sides in 1½ oz butter. Remove and place in casserole dish. Sprinkle an ounce of flour on butter in the pan and cook as a roux. Add ½ pint dry Devon cider, teaspoonful rosemary, salt and freshly milled pepper to taste. Bring to the boil and allow to cook for a minute, stirring constantly. If there does not seem to be enough liquid in which to cook the chops, add a little mild stock or water. Pour over chops and cook in a moderate oven, 350°F, gas 4, for ¾ hour, according to size of chops.

George and Margaret Tonkin

Vivian's Honey Farm, Hatherleigh, Devon.

Note on cooking honey: If honey is heated to a high temperature for more than a few minutes, it loses flavour and important food values. Thus the recipes chosen are those that do not involve such treatment, and, in fact, highlight its flavour. For baking, imported honeys are sufficient. These recipes are well tried.

Devon shares with Yorkshire in having more hives of bees and beekeepers than any other county in Britain. Our fields are not often filled with barley, or droves of combines in summertime and are rarely sprayed with insecticides or weed killers: nor have the hedgerows been pushed flat by bulldozers.

Our climate is well suited to the growing of grass with clover and our agriculture is based mainly on the cows and sheep that feed upon it.

The grass itself produces no nectar for bees, but the clover, filling the pastures to the north of Dartmoor, yields much nectar when we have a warm humid June and July. The clover flowers well, above the grass kept down by the nibbling of sheep or after the first cut of hay.

The numerous hedgerows harbour a variety of nectar-giving plants; the honeysuckle, blackberry, hawthorn and bluebell, that give much added flavour to the pale gold and mild flavoured clover honey.

At present we have some 250 hives in groups over a large area of the county to the north of Dartmoor, and operated from Hatherleigh.

In early August some are taken to the heather covered slopes high up on Dartmoor. There, in all too few good years, the bees gather a strongly perfumed honey much sought after by those who know it.

Our honey is spun out from the combs, and when naturally crystallized to a soft creamy texture, it is bottled.

Honey Junket

1 pint milk   2 oz honey
2 teaspoonsful vanilla flavoured Rennet

Method.   Stir honey into milk and warm to about 104°F. Remove from heat, stir in rennet and leave to set in a cool place. This is delicious served with Devon clotted cream.

Honey Jelly

½ oz gelatine   6 oz clover honey or 4 oz clover
½ pint hot water   honey and 2 oz heather honey
Juice of 1 lemon   1 gill cold water
Chopped apple or orange segments

Method.   Dissolve the gelatine in hot water, add lemon juice and honey and stir till dissolved. Add cold water and fruit and pour into a mould.

Honey Chiffon

1 oz cornflour   2 lemons
2 oz honey   1 oz margarine
2 eggs   2 oz caster sugar

Method.   Grate the rinds of the lemons and squeeze out the juice. Make the juice up to ½ pint with water. Blend the cornflour in a little of the lemon liquid, boil the remaining liquid and pour it over the blended cornflour, stirring all the time. Put the mixture back in the pan and boil for 3 minutes. Add the grated lemon rind and margarine. Allow to cool slightly and add the egg yolks and honey. Whisk the egg whites stiffly, fold in the caster sugar and blend into the lemon mixture. Pour into a mould and leave to set.

Honey Marmalade

1 tin prepared Seville oranges   3½ lb honey
¾ pint water

Method.   Pour oranges, honey and water into a preserving pan and bring to the boil. Boil gently for 15 minutes, stirring continuously, then remove from the heat. Pour into prepared warm jars and cover. Approximate yield 5½ lb.

Mrs R. W. Townsend

Topsham.

Wife of the Treasurer of the Exeter Y.W.C.A.

This recipe was given to me many years ago by a Devonshire country woman and the name is spelt as it sounded to me! She said it was a family dish they always served up when the Vicar came to supper during the Christmas season. It is very good in cold weather and can be made as a small dish for two people, or as a large dish for a hungry family. For this reason, I have given no quantities.

Likky Frizzle

Mashed potatoes   Leeks
Breast of lamb, chopped, but not divided

Method. Line the base and sides of a deep pie-dish or baking tin thickly with mashed potato. Boil and chop the leeks and cover the base with them. Stew the lamb until tender, and then place whole on top of the leeks and potato, and bake in a hot oven until brown and crisp.

             ✧ ✧ ✧

'The history of sheep-grazing, especially for man's use, on the Devon hillsides goes back well into the dim past. Perhaps to the days when Neolithic tribes, driven from the continent by oppressors, brought their sheep and cattle tied by the legs across the English Channel to Britain in dug-out canoes. Here they found heavily wooded lowlands full of wild animals, too dangerous for them to settle, so the rivers were followed up to the open hills, like Dartmoor and Exmoor.

'The importance of the sheep in the economy of Britain has remained ever since, because of their dual value in meat and wool. Sometimes one quality flourished more than the other, as in Medieval times, when merchants of Exeter, Ashburton and similar towns wove woollen cloth and exported it through Topsham, Teignmouth and Dartmouth.

'Devon evolved and established in their own right at least five distinct breeds of sheep, Dartmoor, Exmoorhorn, Devon Longwool, South Devon and Devon Closewool. Each was suited to a locality of the varying conditions found in Devon, including breeds for the rich arable lowlands after deforestation.

'They held their own against all comers until recent times. Now competition with man-made fibres of nylon, etc. is causing the local breeds to be crossed with Northern breeds, like the Border Leicester, which is more disposed to twinning and good mothering, qualities necessary for early fat lamb production. So with less emphasis on wool we see our fields full of clean-faced, clean-legged spring lambs with the pricked-up ears of the Border Leicester.'

H. N. SNOWDON, March 1970.

Mrs E. Tozer

Exeter.

Sheriff's Lady, 1969–70,

The whole dinner is placed in hot oven, is cooked without any attention, and is withdrawn at the end of the specified time ready for serving, with the exception of the sweet. This may be left in the oven (bottom) with gas or heat low to finish cooking or to keep hot as necessary.

Roast Pheasants and Potatoes

1 brace pheasants
2 oz dripping
Slices of fat bacon—approx. 6

1½ lb peeled potatoes cut in half
if large

Method. Cover the breasts of the pheasants with slices of bacon. Season to taste. Place dripping in meat tin in oven when gas is first lighted. When fat is hot add potatoes and baste them. Place the pheasants in the same tin and cover the pheasants with damp greaseproof paper or foil. No further basting required. Place above middle grid. Test with skewer to see if done. Meat should feel tender.

If stuffing is liked, it is better to make it and cook it separately either in a small pie dish covered with foil or a little casserole. It is not advisable to put stuffing in the carcase of the birds.

Bread Sauce

2 oz fresh breadcrumbs (not packet)
½ pint milk

1 small onion stuck with 2 cloves
1 oz butter or margarine

Method. Put breadcrumbs, onion with cloves and seasoning in small fireproof casserole. Pour over milk, cover with lid and place in oven, lowest grid. Before serving remove onion, add butter and mix well.

Braised Brussels Sprouts

2 lb sprouts

½ oz margarine or some bacon
rinds, or butter

Method. Wash and trim sprouts and place in boiling water. Boil for 2 minutes and pour off most of the water. Turn sprouts into a casserole, add salt, pepper, butter or rinds. Shake well, cover with buttered paper and leave in oven on lowest grid.

Cranberry and Apple Tart

1 lb cranberries (tinned ones are good)
Little water, sugar to taste

1 lb cooking apples
12 oz short-crust pastry

Method. Peel, core and cut apples in thick slices. Arrange in a pie dish with the cranberries, with a layer of sugar between the fruit. Add a *little* water. Cover with the pastry. Stand tart in a shallow baking tin, to catch any escaping juice. Grid above lowest one. The oven should be at gas 6 for 45 minutes, 400°F, then turned down to 370°F, gas 5, for ¼ hour.

Sausage Pie

1 medium sized onion
1½ oz butter
12 oz cooked sliced potatoes

12 oz skinless pork sausages
½ lb tomatoes
Salt and pepper

Method. Peel onion and chop finely. Melt half butter in frying pan, add onion and cook gently until tender. Cut each sausage into four pieces, add to the pan and cook for about five minutes, until brown all over. Chop tomatoes, stir them into the sausage and onion and cook, plus seasoning, for a few more minutes. Arrange potato slices on top, brush with remaining softened butter and put under grill to colour the surface. This is good served with shredded lettuce or watercress.

Baked Apple Dumplings and Devonshire Cream

1 lb short crust pastry
Sugar; cloves if liked

6 cooking apples
A little milk for glazing

Method. Roll out pastry and cut into rounds large enough to cover each apple, completely. Peel and core apples. Place one apple on each round of pastry, fill centre with sugar and 1 clove. Brush edges of pastry with milk and seal over apple. Brush outer cover lightly with milk to give a nice golden brown when baked. Place apples, sealed side down on greased baking tray. Bake in middle of oven for 30–45 minutes according to size. Gas 6, 400°F.

Miss Sheila Tracy
Plymouth.
B.B.C. Announcer.

It's probably more Cornish than Devonshire as I got it from my grandmother who was Cornish. It is undoubtedly quite the nicest fruit cake I have ever tasted and I have never had a failure with it.

Rich Fruit Cake

1 lb self-raising flour
½ lb sultanas
¼ lb mixed peel
½ lb granulated sugar
3 eggs
¼ pint milk

¼ flat teaspoon bi-carbonate of
    soda
½ lb currants
2 oz glace cherries
¾ lb butter
4 oz golden syrup

Method. Rub butter into sifted flour and bi-carbonate until it resembles breadcrumbs (as for pastry). Add all dry ingredients and mix well. Then add beaten eggs, syrup and milk. Mix well. Line a 9 inch cake tin with greaseproof paper and bake cake in a pre-heated oven, mark 4, 350°F, for 20 minutes. Then reduce oven heat to mark 2, 300°F, and continue to bake for 2 to 2¼ hours.

Mrs Christopher Tremlett

Lympstone.

Wife of a Topsham Boat Builder.

Who writes, 'I live in a sixteenth-century farm-house, within sight of the River Exe. In the old days the house was used by smugglers. In the attic there is a little window overlooking the river, called the "Smugglers" Look-out.'

Smugglers' Chops—For four people.

4 chump lamb chops	1 small tin sweet red peppers
4 rashers streaky bacon	1 small green pepper
4 lambs' kidneys	Salt and pepper
8 oz small mushrooms	2 tablespoonsful cream
A little oil	Dash of brandy

Method. Fry the chops in a frying pan in the oil until cooked. Meanwhile, de-rind and chop the bacon. Skin, clean and chop the kidneys. Chop the green and red peppers. Slice the mushrooms. When the chops are cooked, transfer them to a casserole dish. Fry the bacon and kidneys. Add the green and red peppers, the mushrooms plus the juice from the tin of red peppers. Season with salt and pepper and when cooked pour over the chops. Cook in a medium oven for 20–30 minutes. Just before serving, add the cream and brandy. Serve with Pommes Anna and green peas.

Pommes Anna

Method. Slice raw old potatoes into ⅛ inch slices. Butter thickly an oven dish, place slices of potatoes, moisten with melted butter, seasoned with salt and pepper and interspersed with re-strained quantities of grated onion. Fill dish, press down, brush with butter and oil mixed and cook slowly for 2–3 hours, gas 2, 300°F. Turn out like a cake. Serve hot sprinkled with chopped parsley.

Mary Tyndale-Biscoe

Parracombe, North Devon.

Mrs Tyndale-Biscoe is a farmer's wife and she sent this 'refreshing and economical Summer Sweet, particularly liked by children'.

Lemon Fluff

3 tablespoonsful semolina	3–5 tablespoonsful sugar
1 lemon, juice and rind	1½ pints water

Method. Put semolina in a bowl with sugar and grated lemon rind (or if preferred rind can be peeled thinly and put in saucepan with water). Mix to a smooth paste with cold water and bring the rest to the boil. Pour this over the mixture in the bowl, transfer to the pan and bring to the boil stirring well until the mixture thickens. Continue to boil for about 5 minutes.

Remove from stove and allow to cool, transferring to bowl. Add the lemon juice and beat well with egg whisk or electric mixer until it changes colour to pure white.

Put in refrigerator for ½–1 hour, then beat well again until stiff. Turn into a glass dish and serve with Devonshire cream.

David Wagner

Exeter.

Mr Wagner took a job as 1st Chef at twenty years of age at the Rock Inn, Haytor, Devon, and is now Chef at the Highwayman's Haunt, Chudleigh. Played Rugger for Exeter.

Tomato and Shredded Egg Soup

Method. Slice 2 onions and sweat off in a little butter until tender. Add tin of tomatoes and enough stock for quantity required, salt and pepper, 1 bay leaf and a little crushed garlic. Bring to boil and simmer for 30 minutes skimming frequently. Sieve and return to pan. Beat 2 eggs together and pass through a strainer into the boiling soup. This gives a shredded look in soup.

Escalope of Pork Favourite

Method. A boned loin of pork for as many as required. De-rind the meat, slice into portions and flatten. (*To flatten any meat out, place meat inside a polythene bag and beat with meat bat. This way meat will not break up.*) Dust the pork with seasoned flour and fry in hot butter both sides. Place on to flat or dish and cover with a slice of ham and then a thick slice of cheese and gratinate under salamander (grill). Serve with tomato and mushrooms and fresh green salad.

Mrs M. L. Walkinton

Ashwell House, Ugbrooke Park, Chudleigh, South Devon.

Wife of a retired Land Agent, now farming, with 65 cows, corn and potatoes, beef, in lovely countryside.

Chartreuse of Devon Salmon

1 quart aspic jelly	3 yolks of hard boiled eggs
1 lb cooked salmon	$\frac{1}{2}$ lemon
6 boned anchovies	$\frac{1}{2}$ wineglass cooking sherry
Salt, pepper, paprika and nutmeg	2 teaspoonsful chutney
1 gill cream	Salad and cucumber

Method. Coat wet plain mould with melted aspic. Set jelly about $\frac{1}{4}$ inch thick in bottom of mould. Decorate with cucumber, setting design with more aspic. Skin and bone fish. Pound with yolks of eggs, anchovies and chutney. Add sherry, lemon juice and 1 cup liquid aspic. Rub this mixture through a sieve. Season and stir in lightly beaten cream. Put half in layer in mould and set in refrigerator. Keep rest of mixture in bowl over saucepan of hot water. Repeat layers of salmon cream and aspic, letting layers set in refrigerator before adding the next. Turn out when set and garnish. Serve with home-made mayonnaise.

Mrs B. White

Redhills, Exeter.

Who came from Spain (La Linea), 27 years ago.

Whitebait Fans—*Suitable for fish course or hors d'oeuvre.*

Method. Wash fish (approx. 12 = 1 oz). Drain, sprinkle with salt and coat lightly with flour. Heat oil in pan until slightly smoking. Pick up 6 or 7 fish, one by one, hold each tail between finger and thumb to make fan shape. Press together; the tails and the flour will 'cement' them. Lower the fans in gently, one by one. Cook 3–4 minutes. Arrange attractively in a small pyramid. Garnish with lemon butterflies (thin slice of lemon cut in half; cut the outer rind of each half and open to form wings), and fresh parsley. Serve with thin slices of brown bread and butter. Serve at once, hot. If necessary they can be kept warm and crisp in a low oven, but uncovered, for about 30 minutes.

Country Omelet—Enough for three.

1 onion	6 tablespoonsful olive oil
1 potato	3 eggs and pinch of salt

Method. Peel and chop the onion and fry in hot oil in omelet pan, preferably non-stick type, 2–3 minutes.

Peel potato and cut into small dice, add to the pan. Continue cooking until potato is tender and onion golden brown (about 20 minutes). Beat the eggs with a pinch of salt and pour into the pan. Stir ingredients lightly together with a fork then leave to settle and cook gently until underside is golden brown. Carefully turn over by slipping omelet on to a plate, then turning it over into the pan to brown other side. Serve immediately with thinly sliced fresh tomatoes.

Variation—For three people.

1½ lb spinach, cooked.	1 onion sliced and cooked in
3 eggs and pinch of salt.	olive oil (6 tablespoonsful) till
Grated cheese to finish.	transparent.

Method. Cook onion, beat the eggs with a pinch of salt. Beat eggs, salt and spinach together, add to onion in pan, leave to settle and cook gently. Proceed as above. Sprinkle grated cheese over and serve.

Rapid Salad—Serves four.

1 small onion chopped fine or spring onion or chives	8 oz cooked potatoes
	Few sprigs parsley
2 hard-boiled eggs	1 can or 7 oz Tuna
2–3 tablespoonsful olive oil or melted butter	A few green olives
	Seasoning and lemon to taste

Method. Cut the potatoes into cubes. Chop the hard boiled eggs. Slice olives and flake the tuna. Mix all ingredients well together and moisten with olive oil or melted butter and lemon juice. Season.

White Bread

Sufficient for two small loaves, in two 1lb loaf tins.

1 lb strong plain flour
1 teaspoonful sugar
½ oz fresh yeast
½ oz melted butter or 1 tablespoonful oil

1½ teaspoonsful salt
½ pint warm water (approx., see note)
Warm mixing bowl

Method. 1. Sieve flour and salt into warm bowl. Keep warm.

2. Soften yeast with a little warm water and sugar, and when blended, add the rest of the warm water.

3. Make a well in the flour, and pour in fat and yeast water mixture.

4. Beat with a claw-like hand, loose at the wrist, bringing in the sides of the dough to the middle; doing this for about 10–15 minutes makes the gluten elastic, as well as spreading the yeast. When ready, the dough looks silky, feels firm and elastic, and is no longer sticky.

5. Cover with a greased paper and clean tea towel or oiled polythene cover. Leave to double its size, in a warm place.

6. Turn on to a warm surface, and with floured hands, knead, bringing sides into middle, and pushing down with the fist.

7. Divide the dough, and put into greased tins or pots. Leave to rise in a warm place until almost to the top, covered as before.

8. Bake in centre of oven 450°F, gas 8, for 5 minutes, and reduce to 425°F, gas 7, for about 30 minutes.

Tap under the loaf, which sounds hollow when done; if not quite ready, remove from tins and return to the oven for a few minutes: this also gives a crisper finish.

Brush *before* baking with (a) water, (b) for a hard crust, salt and water, (c) milk, or

Brush *after* baking, with (a) milk or egg and sprinkle with poppy seed or (b) rub over with butter paper.

Tomato Bread *Use the recipe for White Bread, but use ¼ pint warm water, and add 5 oz tomato purée, to mix the dough. Add a little paprika, about 1 teaspoonful, if liked. Proceed as above. This is delicious for savouries, for sandwiches or for breakfast.*

Notes: Yeast will keep wrapped, in the refrigerator for 2–3 weeks, and it is economical to buy 1 lb at the time from Health Food shops. Dried yeast can be bought in 1 lb containers and will keep several months. If dried yeast is used for the above recipe, dissolve 1 teaspoonful sugar in ½ pint warm water, sprinkle on 2 level teaspoonsful dried yeast, and leave to froth for about 10–15 minutes. About ⅔ cold to ⅓ boiling water gives the right temperature. Fat can be omitted: bread keeps better with it, but the crust is not so crisp. Two 5 inch clay flower pots can be used instead of tins, to give an 'old-fashioned' bread flavour; they are scrubbed as soon as bought, dried, brushed with oil, and baked for 30 minutes before being used for the first time, then greased as usual.

Mr and Mrs Richard Whiteway
Whimple, Exeter.

Pork and Apples

4 lean pork chops	4 eating apples
1 teaspoonful chopped sage	Salt and pepper
½ pint apple juice, Whiteways, Devon	1 dessertspoonful olive oil

Method. Brown chops in oil, add peeled sliced apples, sage, apple juice and seasoning. Cover and simmer for 20 minutes, turning chops once. Serve with pan juices in the mashed potatoes.

Orchard Chicken

1 boiling fowl	1 large onion
1 lb eating apples	Salt and pepper
1 pint apple juice	

Method. Stuff bird with peeled and cored apples and sprinkle with salt and pepper. Slice onion and put into casserole, put bird on top and pour on apple juice. Cook at 300°F, gas 2, for 4 hours. If a thicker sauce is liked, beat up 2 raw egg yolks, pour on some chicken stock, stirring well, but do not re-heat once the eggs are in the sauce.

Cyder Baked Ham

½ pint strong still cyder	5 lb piece of ham
2 onions	3 carrots
3 sticks celery	12 cloves
Demerara sugar	

Method. Soak ham overnight, drain off water and put ham in pan with enough water to cover and with vegetables cut in small pieces. Simmer gently for 75 minutes and then remove pan from heat. Leave ham in water for 30 minutes, drain and put in baking tin. Lift off skin and stud fat with cloves. Spread with sugar and pour cyder over ham. Bake for 40 minutes at 350°F, gas 4, basting three times. Leave on a rack to cool and baste two or three times more as meat cools. Carve when cold. Serve to family with salad and jacket baked potatoes or as a party dish for up to twenty people.

Bacon with Whiteway's Devon Cyder Sauce

1 pint light still cyder	3 lb joint bacon
8 small peeled onions	4 medium eating apples
1 oz plain flour	1 tablespoonful redcurrant jelly

Method. Soak bacon in cold water overnight if necessary. Drain and put into large casserole with cyder and onions. Cover and cook for 1½ hours at 350°F, gas 4. Remove from oven and turn bacon over and arrange cored but not peeled apples round bacon. Return to oven for 30 minutes. Put bacon on serving dish with onions and apples. Pour juices into a saucepan and add flour mixed to a smooth paste with a little water and the redcurrant jelly. Bring to the boil, stirring all the time and boil for 3 minutes. Serve in a sauceboat. Serve as a family meal or to about twelve people as a party dish.

114

Phyllis Whitmarsh

Yelverton.

Wife of Gerald Whitmarsh, Esq., Chairman of Devon County Council.

Salmon Mould

½ oz gelatine, dissolved in
   3 tablespoonsful water
8 oz cooked salmon
1½ tablespoonsful sugar
½ teaspoonful dry mustard
½ pint warm milk

Yolks 2 eggs
½ teaspoonful salt
¼ tablespoonful flour
1½ tablespoonsful melted butter
2 tablespoonsful vinegar or
   lemon juice

Method. Mash salmon and remove bones. Warm milk and melt butter gently. Beat egg yolks and add to butter and milk. Beat together. Mix sugar, salt, flour and mustard. On to this pour a little of the egg mixture and make a smooth paste. Add remainder and stir until smooth. Put in double saucepan over boiling water and stir mixture until it is thick enough to coat spoon. Add vinegar or lemon juice. Remove from heat and let cool while you dissolve the gelatine. Stir gently into egg mixture, and add mashed salmon. Stir well and pour into dish. Allow to set. Eat cold with salad.

Chicken Casserole

4 chicken joints
1 onion
2 rashers streaky bacon
¾ pint chicken stock

1½ oz bacon fat or butter
1 stick celery
1 oz plain flour, salt, pepper
3 tomatoes

Method. Fry chicken slowly for about 10 minutes in fat. Put in casserole. Add finely chopped onion, sliced celery and chopped bacon, to the fat in the frying pan, and cook gently for several minutes. Sprinkle in flour, salt and pepper, and cook a minute, add stock and stir until boiling. Add skinned tomatoes, pour over chicken in casserole. Cover and cook for 40–50 minutes, 350°F, gas 4.

Devonshire Splits

12 oz flour
¼ teaspoon salt
2 teaspoons baking powder

2 oz butter
¾ teacup milk
½ oz caster sugar

Method. Rub fat into flour. Add dry ingredients. Make a dough with milk. Form into rounds and bake 15–20 minutes, 400°F, gas 6. Serve with home-made strawberry jam, and plenty of Devonshire cream.

Mrs R. C. Wield

Chudleigh, near Newton Abbot.

Has spent twenty-one years in the Hospital Car Service—one of the longest serving members.

'Little-Cooking' Leek Pie—For 4-6 people.

¼ lb chopped cooked ham or bacon
¼ lb grated cheddar cheese
1 large can cream of chicken or
  mushroom soup

1½ lb potatoes
2 large leeks (about 1 lb)
Salt and pepper to taste

Method. Peel the potatoes and parboil in salted water about 15 minutes. Trim tops of leeks, wash and cut in half lengthwise; place on top of potatoes, allowing 10 minutes to parboil. Drain the vegetables, cut the leeks in half and the potatoes into ½ inch slices. Put them into a greased ovenproof dish, sprinkle with salt and pepper. Add chopped ham or bacon and pour the soup over. Top with grated cheese, cook at about 425°F, or gas mark 7-8, for 20 minutes. Serve piping hot. If desired, the top can be grilled brown for a few minutes. Very little cooking needed.

Lemon Cream

Rind of 1 lemon
3 oz caster sugar
½ pint whipping cream
¼ cup warm water

Juice of 2 lemons
3 egg yolks, 3 egg whites
2½ teaspoonsful gelatine

Method. Soften gelatine in the ¼ cup of warm water. Whisk sugar with lemon juice and rind and egg yolks. Add gelatine and whisk until stiff. Beat cream until thick and add to lemon mixture. Whisk egg whites until you can turn the bowl upside down without them falling out and fold into lemon mixture. ¼ pint of extra whipping cream on top makes a real 'party' pudding. *Should have said pour into a pretty dish!*

Mrs G. H. Wilkinson

Pennsylvania Park, Exeter.

Apple Cake

8 oz self-raising flour
4 oz granulated sugar
1 egg beaten in a little milk
Small pinch salt

4 oz butter or 2 oz lard and 2 oz
  margarine
2 or 3 medium sized apples,
  Bramley if possible

Method. Rub fat into flour, add sugar and apple diced. Mix in egg and milk with a fork. Grease well a shallow tin, and put mixture in. Bake 350°F–375°F, gas 4-5, about 40 minutes. Serve hot, cut into fingers, dusted with caster sugar, and a knob of butter on each portion.

W. R. (Tug) Wilson

*Sometime County Organiser for the Devon County Federation
of Young Farmers' Clubs.*

Kenton Chicken

1 chicken (4 lb and over)
1 medium sized onion
2–3 stalks celery, sliced
1½ wineglass champagne/cider
2½ fluid oz double cream

1½ oz butter
2 medium sized cooking apples
1 tablespoonful flour
¾ pint jellied stock
Chopped parsley

Garnish:

2 Cox's apples
Caster sugar

1 oz butter

Method. Brown chicken slowly all over in the butter, in flameproof casserole. Meanwhile quarter, core and slice the apples. When chicken is browned, take out of casserole and put in onion, apples and celery and sauté gently for 5 to 6 minutes. Remove from heat and stir in flour, add wine and stock. Bring to the boil and season, and turn out into bowl. Joint chicken and return to casserole. Pour over sauce, and cover with foil and lid. Cook in oven or on top of stove for 55 or 60 minutes, according to size of bird, at 350°F, or gas 4.

While chicken is cooking prepare apple garnish. Wipe apples, cut ¼ inch to ½ inch strips. Take out core with sharp knife or apple corer. Fry rings in butter and dust well with sugar. Do this at full heat for 1½ to 2 minutes. When brown keep hot on greased plate. When chicken is tender, take out of casserole and strain sauce, pushing as much vegetable through strainer as possible. Put in saucepan, adjust seasoning, and boil up till syrupy. Add cream, whisking it well in. Spoon enough sauce to cover chicken portions, garnish with apple. Serve rest of sauce separately (it is too good to waste on serving dish!).

Fried Bread Sauce

2 rashers lean bacon, cut into small
  pieces
Parsley, lemon juice, and 1 cup stock

1 shallot finely chopped
1 cup breadcrumbs
Butter and oil

Method. Fry breadcrumbs in oil and butter (put aside). Fry the bacon and shallot until cooked. Add stock, boil, and simmer for 10 minutes. Add fried breadcrumbs, chopped parsley, and lemon juice to taste. Add salt if necessary, and serve.

Slices of tomatoes, sprinkled with sugar, and grilled, give a good colour, when added to gravy.

A. N. Winckworth

Dunchideock House, near Exeter.

'Dunchideock has been famous for centuries for its treacle, mined from the local theriaciferous rocks. A recent article in a scientific journal described the product as having a 'smooth, strong, distinctive flavour'. It is essential that the following recipe should be made only with genuine Dunchideock treacle'. The editor of this book feels bound to point out that other treacle will do. It is perhaps due to Lewis Carroll's reference to a treacle well that supplies have become so elusive; becoming, perhaps due to the demand in the nineteenth century, almost exhausted.

Dunchideock Treacle Scones

8 oz flour
2 tablespoonsful Dunchideock treacle
(see above note)
1 teaspoonful mixed spice (cinnamon, ginger, etc.)

1½ oz butter
1 oz sugar
½ teaspoonful cream of tartar
½ teaspoonful bi-carbonate soda

Method. After mixing other ingredients, add the treacle after it has been warmed. Knead well and place on floured tin in shapes and sizes required. Glazing with beaten egg improves the appearance. Bake in a moderate oven for 20 minutes. Serve very new, preferably before becoming cold.

Women's Royal Voluntary Service

County Borough Office, 55 Longbrook Street, Exeter.

Black Coffee Jelly

Method. Dissolve ½ oz of gelatine in 1 pint of strong, unsweetened black coffee and pour into a ring mould. Turn out when set and fill centre with sweetened cream.

❖ ❖ ❖

W.R.V.S. covers a wide field of work for the community and co-operates with local authorities in undertaking a great deal of welfare work for Hospitals, Children, Old People and H.M. Forces both at home and abroad. In order to give efficient help in any local emergency all W.R.V.S. members undertake a simple training.

Dr Joyce Youings

University of Exeter.

Chairman of the National Trust, Exeter Centre.

Dr Youings, born and brought up in Barnstaple, now lives at Thorverton. She is Reader in Tudor History at the University, and Warden of one of the Halls of Residence for Women.

'*I am very fond of food, but am no cook. I do, however, have a favourite dish which even I can manage, namely hogs pudding and laver. Very good hogs puddings are available in Exeter, but it is not easy to find laver. Keep asking!*'

Hogs Pudding and Laver

Hogs puddings are made of pork and oatmeal, well-seasoned, and are sold, like sausages, in skins. They should be fried or baked in the oven in a little dripping and should be encouraged to ooze a little from their skins so that they become crisp at the edges.

Laver is a special variety of slimy seaweed which grows, and is gathered, among other places, on the rocks of North Devon. It is sold, usually by fishmongers, already cooked and free of sand. It should be heated, also with a little dripping, in a saucepan and needs a little salt and pepper. With the puddings and laver, one should serve mashed potato and mashed swede turnip, but for a breakfast dish, simply fried potatoes with perhaps a rasher of bacon.

Devonshire Black and White Puddings, are made with liver, beef, hearts and groats. Blood is added to the black puddings, and omitted from the white. They are sold ready cooked, and to heat them, slice them in half lengthwise. They can be fried, in which case cover them, as they 'hop', or they can be grilled.

Stir-fry Liver—*A quick meal.*

½ lb liver
1 tablespoonful Soy sauce, or
   1 teaspoonful Marmite
½ teaspoonful mace
2 tablespoonsful cider
4 oz Patna long-grained rice

1 level tablespoonful cornflour
½ level teaspoonful ground ginger
½ level teaspoonful salt
Crushed clove of garlic, if liked
3 tablespoonsful oil for frying
Garnish: lemon, tomato, peanuts

Method. Slice liver very thinly with a sharp knife. Mix cornflour, Soy, ginger, mace, salt, garlic and cider in a basin, and add the liver. Leave ½ hour before required.

Cook rice. This can be done earlier, placed in a colander, and left over a pan of gently steaming water, covered with a cloth. Make the rice into a ring on a hot dish.

Heat the oil in a frying pan, and tip the liver, etc. into it. Stir with a wooden spoon over high heat for 3 minutes. Place into ring of rice, and garnish.

Beef may be used in place of liver, in which case cut very thinly, across the fibres.

Mrs A. Young

Hookhills Road, Paignton.

'My husband, in a busy profession, is very good at making this bread also ... He will not eat any other kind except when away from home!'

100% **Wholemeal Bread**

3 lb wholemeal flour
2 oz fresh yeast or 1 oz dried yeast
1¾ pints warm water

1 oz salt
2 teaspoonsful soft brown sugar

Method. Mix flour and salt in bowl, place in simmering oven (Aga) or a warm place. Crumble yeast into a small basin, add two teaspoonsful soft brown sugar and ¼ pint warm water. Place in warmth beside flour. Set timer for 10 minutes.

Grease loaf tins generously with roast dripping or similar cooking fat. Flour well. (I use 5 one pound tins for this quantity.) When 10 minutes have expired, mix yeast mixture into flour plus 1½ pints warm water. Mix well until a smooth wettish dough with a smooth silky finish results.

Divide dough amongst tins and place to rise in simmering oven (Aga) or warm place. Set timer for about 20 minutes. (This can be done in the airing cupboard, but takes longer.)

If dough has risen well to top of tins, transfer immediately to hot oven (Aga), gas 7, 425°F. If not fully risen, leave a few minutes longer.

Bake for ¾ hour, moving round if necessary. Turn out loaves immediately when done and cool on a wire tray.

ACKNOWLEDGEMENTS

The editor thanks all those who have helped in the making of this book: friends who have given their time, Mr D. J. Morgan, ASTD, of Messrs James Townsend and Sons Ltd, Exeter, Messrs Sydney Lee (Exeter) Limited and the publishers of *Devon Life* who have kindly allowed us to use some of their blocks.

We gratefully acknowledge permission given by Miss Bradbeer to use any passages from her book, *The Story of the Manor and Port of Topsham*; by Professor W. G. Hoskins to use 'what we like' from his many books; by Mr Nigel Nicolson to use an extract from V. Sackville West's *The Land*, and by Mr H. N. Snowdon to use some of his notes on rural Devonshire.